UNLOCKING THE POWER OF BAOFENG RADIO BIBLE

Guerrilla Communication: A Guide to Understanding Your Two-way Radio for Everyday Use

Michael Joe Wisdom

Copyright © 2024 by Michael Joe Wisdom

All rights reserved. No part of this publication may be reproduced, distributed or transmitted in any form or by any means, including photocopying, recording, or other electronic or mechanical methods, without the prior written permission of the publisher, except in the case of brief quotations embodied in critical reviews and certain other noncommercial uses permitted by copyright law.

Table of Contents

INTRODUCTION   **1**
    Why Choose Baofeng Radios?   7
CHAPTER 1   **12**
Getting Started With Baofeng Radios   **12**
    Unpacking Your Baofeng: Key Components and Features   12
    Basic Operation   19
    Essential Accessories for Enhancing Your Experience   24
CHAPTER 2   **32**
Mastering Basic Functions   **32**
    Understanding Frequency: VHF vs. UHF   32
    Programming Channels Manually   37
    Using Repeater Channels for Extended Range   42
    Scanning and Monitoring Multiple Channels   47
CHAPTER 3   **54**
Advanced Programming and Customization   **54**
    Using Chirp Software for Programming   54
    Creating and Managing Channel Lists   60
    Setting Up CTCSS/DCS Codes for Privacy   67
    Configuring Dual Watch and Dual Standby Modes   73
CHAPTER 4   **82**
Practical Applications for Everyday Use   **82**
    Communicating in Urban Environments   82
    Using Baofeng Radios for Outdoor Adventures   88

Coordination in Events 95
Enhancing Safety and Security 101
CHAPTER 5 **108**
Emergency Preparedness and Disaster Communication **108**
    The Role of Radios in Emergency Situations 108
    Setting Up an Emergency Communication Plan 115
    Communicating During Natural Disasters 122
    Staying Informed: Monitoring Emergency Broadcasts and Weather Channels 127
CHAPTER 6 **132**
Legal and Ethical Considerations **132**
    Understanding FCC Regulations and Licensing Requirements 132
    Ethical Use of Two-Way Radios 140
    Privacy Concerns and Best Practices 146
    Avoiding Interference with Public Services 151
CHAPTER 7 **158**
Troubleshooting and Maintenance **158**
    Common Issues and Quick Fixes 158
    Maintaining Battery Health and Longevity 163
    Cleaning and Caring for Your Baofeng Radio 168
    Upgrading Firmware and Software 173
CHAPTER 8 **180**
Building a Community Network **180**
    Connecting with Local Radio Enthusiasts 180
    Participating in Ham Radio Clubs and Networks 186

Organizing Community Drills and Training
Sessions   193
Online Resources and Forums for Continuous
Learning   200
CHAPTER 9   208
Enhancing Range and Performance   208
Optimizing Antenna Placement and Selection
208
Using Signal Boosters and Repeaters   214
Environmental Factors Affecting Signal Strength
221
DIY Projects for Improving Radio Performance
227
CHAPTER 10   234
Future Trends and Innovations in Radio
Communication   234
The Impact of Digital Modes on Two-Way
Radios   234
Integration with Smartphones and Other
Devices   240
Emerging Technologies in Emergency
Communication   247
The Future of Baofeng and Other Affordable
Radio Solutions   253
CONCLUSION   260

INTRODUCTION

Radio communication has come a long way since its inception, playing a crucial role in how we connect over long distances. It all started in the late 19th century when scientists began experimenting with wireless signals. One of the pioneers was Guglielmo Marconi, an Italian inventor who is often credited with inventing the radio. In the 1890s, Marconi successfully sent wireless signals over a distance, and by 1901, he made the first transatlantic radio transmission from England to Newfoundland.

The journey of radio communication began with the discovery of electromagnetic waves by James Clerk Maxwell in the 1860s. These waves, which include visible light, radio waves and X-rays, travel through space and can carry information. Heinrich Hertz furthered Maxwell's work in the 1880s by demonstrating the existence of these waves, thus paving the way for practical applications.

Marconi's early experiments used Morse code, a system of dots and dashes representing letters and numbers. This system allowed for simple messages to be sent wirelessly, a breakthrough for communication over long distances, especially for ships at sea. Before radio, ships relied on visual signals like flags or lanterns, which were limited by distance and visibility. Radio waves could travel much farther and in any weather condition, making maritime communication much safer.

In the early 20th century, radio technology continued to evolve. Reginald Fessenden, a Canadian inventor, made a significant contribution by transmitting the first audio radio broadcast in 1906. He sent out a Christmas Eve broadcast featuring music and speech, marking a shift from simple Morse code to more complex audio signals. This breakthrough meant that voice and music could be sent wirelessly, opening up new possibilities for radio as a medium for entertainment and information.

The development of the vacuum tube by Lee De Forest in 1906 was another critical advancement. Vacuum tubes amplified weak signals, making it possible to broadcast radio signals over even greater distances. This innovation led to the establishment of the first radio stations in the 1920s. KDKA in Pittsburgh, Pennsylvania, is often cited as the world's first commercial radio station, starting regular broadcasts in 1920. Radio quickly became a popular medium for news, music and entertainment, reaching millions of people in their homes.

During World War II, radio communication proved essential for military operations. It allowed for real-time communication between troops, ships and aircraft, significantly improving coordination and effectiveness. The use of radio for propaganda and information dissemination also became widespread, with broadcasts being used to influence public opinion and morale on both sides of the conflict.

After the war, radio technology continued to advance. The invention of the transistor in 1947 by John Bardeen, Walter Brattain and William Shockley revolutionized radio communication. Transistors replaced bulky vacuum tubes, making radios smaller, more portable and more reliable. This led to the proliferation of portable radios, which became a common household item in the 1950s and 1960s.

The 20th century also saw the rise of different types of radio communication, such as frequency modulation (FM) and amplitude modulation (AM). AM radio, which modulates the amplitude of the signal, was the standard for early radio broadcasts. FM radio, developed by Edwin Armstrong in the 1930s, modulates the frequency of the signal and offers better sound quality and less interference. FM radio became popular for music broadcasts, while AM remained dominant for news and talk shows.

The introduction of satellite technology in the latter half of the 20th century marked another significant leap in radio communication. Satellites allowed for global broadcasting, enabling signals to be sent around the world. This technology not only enhanced international communication but also improved services like weather forecasting, navigation, and television broadcasting.

In the late 20th and early 21st centuries, digital technology began to transform radio communication. Digital radio, including satellite radio and internet radio, offered improved sound quality and a wider range of channels. Digital communication protocols like Digital Mobile Radio (DMR) and Project 25 (P25) became standard for public safety and professional use, providing clearer and more reliable communication.

One of the most significant recent developments in radio communication is the integration of radios with other digital devices. Modern two-way radios, like the Baofeng radios, combine traditional radio technology with digital features, making them versatile tools for both everyday use and emergency preparedness. These radios can be programmed with multiple channels, use digital codes for secure communication and even integrate with GPS for location tracking.

Today, radio communication is an essential part of our lives, used in everything from personal communication devices to emergency services, aviation and maritime operations. The evolution of radio from simple wireless signals to sophisticated digital communication systems is a testament to human ingenuity and the ongoing quest to connect over distances.

This rich history underscores the importance of radio communication and its role in shaping our world. From Marconi's early experiments to the advanced digital radios of today, each milestone represents a leap forward in our ability to communicate across vast distances. As technology continues to evolve, radio communication will undoubtedly remain a vital tool, adapting to meet the needs of an ever-connected world.

Why Choose Baofeng Radios?

Baofeng radios are a popular choice for many people who need reliable and efficient communication tools. One of the main reasons people prefer Baofeng radios is their affordability. Unlike many other two-way radios, Baofeng models are budget-friendly, making them accessible to a wide range of users, from hobbyists to emergency preparedness enthusiasts. Despite their low cost, these radios offer a robust set of features that rival more expensive models.

Versatility is another significant advantage of Baofeng radios. They are designed to work in various environments and situations. Whether you are using them for outdoor activities like hiking, camping, or boating or for coordinating events such as festivals and sports activities, Baofeng radios can handle the job. They operate on both VHF and UHF frequencies, which means they can be used in urban areas with lots of buildings and in open spaces where long-range communication is needed. This dual-band capability makes them incredibly flexible and suitable for many different scenarios.

User-friendliness is also a key feature of Baofeng radios. They are designed to be easy to use, even for beginners. The controls are straightforward, with clear labels and a simple interface that makes learning to operate the radio quick and easy. Many models come with a comprehensive manual that guides users through setup and basic operations. Additionally, there are numerous online resources, including videos and forums, where users can find help and advice from a community of experienced users.

Another benefit of Baofeng radios is their programmability. Users can program channels and frequencies manually or use software to customize their radios to meet specific needs. This feature is particularly useful for those who need to set up multiple channels for different purposes, such as coordinating a team during an event or monitoring various frequencies during an emergency. The ability to program the radio adds a layer of customization that enhances its functionality.

Baofeng radios also come with several practical features that enhance their usability. Many models include a built-in flashlight, which can be incredibly handy in low-light situations. They also have an emergency alarm function that can be activated to alert others in case of danger. These additional features make Baofeng radios not just communication devices but also valuable tools for safety and convenience.

Durability is another strong point. Baofeng radios are built to withstand rough conditions. They are made with sturdy materials that can endure drops and bumps, making them suitable for outdoor and rugged use. This durability ensures that your radio will last longer and continue to perform well, even in challenging environments.

The battery life of Baofeng radios is also commendable. They are equipped with long-lasting batteries that can keep the radio operational for extended periods. This is particularly important in situations where you might not have immediate access to charging facilities, such as during a camping trip or an emergency. Having a reliable power source means you can depend on your radio when you need it most.

Baofeng radios are widely used by amateur radio enthusiasts and professionals alike. This widespread use has created a large community of users who share tips, programming guides and other helpful information. Being part of such a community can be incredibly beneficial, especially for new users who are just learning how to get the most out of their radios.

Baofeng radios stand out because they are affordable, versatile, user-friendly, programmable, durable and equipped with practical features. These qualities make them an excellent choice for anyone needing a reliable communication tool, whether for everyday use, outdoor adventures or emergency situations.

CHAPTER 1

Getting Started With Baofeng Radios

Unpacking Your Baofeng: Key Components and Features

When you first open the box of a Baofeng radio, you will find several components that are essential for its operation. Each part has a specific role and together they ensure that your radio works effectively. Understanding these components and their features will help you get started with using your Baofeng radio confidently.

First, you will see the Baofeng radio itself. This is the main device and the most important part of the package. The radio has several buttons, a display screen, an antenna connection point, and ports for accessories. The body of the radio is typically made from durable plastic to withstand everyday use and potential drops. The display screen shows important information like the current channel, frequency, and battery status.

Next, you will find the antenna. The antenna is crucial for transmitting and receiving signals. It usually screws into the top of the radio. Some models come with a basic antenna, but you can also purchase more advanced antennas to improve the radio's range and performance. The antenna helps in picking up signals from other radios and broadcasting your signal over a distance.

Included in the box is the battery. Baofeng radios typically use rechargeable lithium-ion batteries. These batteries are known for their long life and reliability. You will need to attach the battery to the back of the radio. Before using the radio for the first time, it's a good idea to charge the battery fully to ensure maximum usage time.

The box also contains a charger, which is used to recharge the battery. Baofeng radios usually come with a desktop charger, where you place the radio in a cradle to charge. Some models may also include a USB charging cable that can be connected to a computer or a power adapter. This makes it convenient to charge the radio at home or on the go.

Another important component is the belt clip. The belt clip attaches to the back of the radio, allowing you to clip it onto your belt or bag for easy carrying. This is especially useful if you need to keep your hands free while using the radio. The belt clip is usually made of sturdy plastic and is easy to attach and detach.

You will also find an earpiece with a built-in microphone. This accessory is useful for hands-free communication. The earpiece plugs into the side of the radio, and you can use it to listen to messages and talk without holding the radio to your mouth. This is particularly helpful in situations where you need to be discreet or when you're in a noisy environment.

A wrist strap is another component included in the box. The wrist strap attaches to the radio, making it easier to carry and less likely to be dropped. It's a simple but effective accessory that adds to the convenience of using your Baofeng radio.

Additionally, there is usually a user manual included in the package. The manual provides detailed instructions on how to set up and use your radio. It includes diagrams and explanations of each button and feature, making it easier for you to understand how to operate the radio. The manual is an important resource, especially for beginners.

Now, let's talk about some of the primary features of the Baofeng radio itself. One of the standout features is the dual-band capability. This means the radio can operate on two different frequency bands, VHF (Very High Frequency) and UHF (Ultra High

Frequency). This dual-band feature allows for greater flexibility in communication, as you can switch between bands depending on your needs and environment.

The Baofeng radio also has a built-in flashlight. This can be very handy in dark or low-light situations, such as during a nighttime hike or a power outage. The flashlight is usually located at the top of the radio and can be easily turned on and off with a dedicated button.

Another useful feature is the emergency alarm function. This can be activated to alert others if you are in danger or need immediate assistance. When the alarm is triggered, the radio emits a loud sound to draw attention, which can be crucial in emergency situations.

The radio's keypad allows you to manually enter frequencies and channels. This gives you the flexibility to tune into specific frequencies and customize your communication settings. The keypad also includes buttons for adjusting the volume, changing channels and accessing various menu options.

The display screen on the Baofeng radio is another important feature. It shows critical information such as the current channel, frequency and battery level. Some models also display additional information like the signal strength and whether the radio is in transmit or receive mode. The screen is usually backlit, making it easy to read in both bright and dim conditions.

Baofeng radios also have programmable memory channels. This feature allows you to save frequently used frequencies and channels for quick access. You can program these channels manually or use software to load them into the radio. This is particularly useful if you regularly communicate on specific frequencies or need to switch between channels quickly.

In addition to these features, Baofeng radios often come with various scanning functions. Scanning allows the radio to search through a range of frequencies or channels to find active transmissions. This is helpful for monitoring multiple frequencies and staying informed about what's happening around you.

Baofeng radios are known for their durability and reliability. They are built to withstand tough conditions, making them suitable for outdoor adventures, emergency situations and daily use. The combination of affordability, versatile features and robust design makes Baofeng radios a great choice for anyone needing a dependable communication tool.

By understanding the components and primary features of your Baofeng radio, you can make the most of this powerful device and ensure effective communication in a variety of situations.

Basic Operation

Using a Baofeng radio for the first time can be exciting and straightforward. Knowing how to perform basic operations like turning on the radio, selecting channels and adjusting the volume is essential. This guide will help you understand these fundamental steps.

To turn on your Baofeng radio, locate the power/volume knob. This knob is typically found on the top of the radio. It serves two purposes: turning the radio on and off, and controlling the volume. To turn on the radio, twist the knob clockwise until you hear a click. The display screen should light up, indicating that the radio is now on. You might also hear a welcome message or beep, which confirms that the device is operational.

Once the radio is on, you can adjust the volume using the same knob. Continue twisting the knob clockwise to increase the volume. If the volume gets too loud, twist it counterclockwise to lower it.

Finding the right volume level is important, especially in noisy environments or when you need to listen carefully to incoming transmissions. Remember, the same knob will also be used to turn off the radio by twisting it fully counterclockwise until you hear a click.

Selecting a channel is the next step. Channels are pre-programmed frequencies that you can switch between to communicate with different people or groups. To select a channel, you will use the keypad and the display screen. On the side of the radio, there is a button labeled "VFO/MR" (Variable Frequency Oscillator/Memory Recall). Press this button to switch between frequency mode (where you can manually enter a frequency) and memory mode (where you select from pre-programmed channels).

When in memory mode, use the up and down arrow keys on the keypad to scroll through the channels. Each channel will have a corresponding number, and the display screen will show the channel number and its associated frequency. Scroll through the channels until you find the one you need. To quickly jump to a specific channel, you can directly enter the channel number using the keypad. For instance, if you want to go to channel 5, just press the number 5 on the keypad.

In frequency mode, you can manually enter the frequency you want to tune into. This mode is useful if you know the exact frequency you need to communicate on or if you're searching for a specific signal. To enter a frequency, use the keypad to type in the numbers directly. For example, if you want to tune into 145.500 MHz, just type 145500. The display will update to show the entered frequency, and the radio will switch to it.

Additionally, many Baofeng radios come with a scanning feature. Scanning allows the radio to automatically search through available channels or frequencies to find active transmissions. To activate the scan function, look for the "SCAN" button or menu option, usually accessible by pressing the "MENU" button and navigating through the options. Once you activate scanning, the radio will start cycling through channels or frequencies and stop when it detects an active signal. This is useful for monitoring multiple channels or finding conversations in your area.

Another important aspect of channel selection is setting up privacy codes, known as CTCSS (Continuous Tone-Coded Squelch System) or DCS (Digital-Coded Squelch). These codes help ensure that you only hear transmissions from radios using the same code, reducing interference from other users on the same frequency. To set a CTCSS or DCS code, press the "MENU" button, scroll to the appropriate menu item (usually labeled as "T-CTCS" for transmit CTCSS or "R-DCS" for receive DCS), select it, and then use the keypad to enter the desired code. Press the "MENU" button again to confirm your selection.

Baofeng radios also allow you to store your favorite channels in memory for quick access. To save a channel, first ensure you are on the desired frequency or channel. Press the "MENU" button, navigate to the "MEM-CH" (memory channel) option, and select it. Use the keypad to choose a memory slot where you want to save this channel. Press "MENU" again to save it. You can now quickly access this saved channel by switching to memory mode and selecting the corresponding slot number.

Lastly, understanding the dual watch or dual standby feature can enhance your communication experience. This feature allows you to monitor two channels simultaneously. To activate dual watch, press the "MENU" button, find the "TDR" (dual receive) option, and select it. Enable this feature, and the radio will alternate between the two channels, stopping on any channel that receives a transmission. This is particularly useful if you need to keep track of communications on two different frequencies without constantly switching back and forth.

By following these steps, you can effectively operate your Baofeng radio, making sure it meets your communication needs. These basic operations; turning the radio on, selecting channels and adjusting the volume are the foundation of using your Baofeng radio efficiently. As you become more familiar with these functions, you'll find it easier to explore and utilize the additional features your radio offers, ensuring you stay connected in various situations.

Essential Accessories for Enhancing Your Experience

Using Baofeng radios can be greatly enhanced with the right accessories. These accessories can improve the radio's performance, increase its functionality, and make it more convenient to use. Here are some essential accessories for Baofeng radios and how they can enhance your experience.

One of the most important accessories is a high-quality antenna. The standard antenna that comes with your Baofeng radio is functional, but upgrading to a better antenna can significantly improve your signal range and clarity. A popular choice is the Nagoya NA-771 antenna, known for its extended range and durability. This antenna can be easily attached to your radio and will help you communicate more effectively over longer distances, making it ideal for outdoor adventures and emergency situations.

An earpiece with a built-in microphone is another useful accessory. It allows for hands-free operation, which is especially helpful when you need to keep your hands free for other tasks. The earpiece fits comfortably in your ear, and the microphone is positioned near your mouth, making it easy to speak without holding the radio. This setup is perfect for busy environments or when you need to be discreet. Additionally, earpieces often come with a push-to-talk (PTT) button, which makes transmitting messages even more convenient.

External microphones, also known as speaker microphones, are valuable for users who need to communicate frequently and clearly. These microphones clip onto your clothing and have a built-in speaker, allowing you to hear and speak without having to hold the radio. They are especially useful for professionals like security personnel, event coordinators and outdoor enthusiasts. The Baofeng speaker microphone is a popular option, providing clear audio and easy access to the PTT button.

A programming cable is essential for those who want to customize their Baofeng radios. This cable connects your radio to a computer, allowing you to use software to program frequencies, channels and settings. Using software like CHIRP, you can quickly and easily set up your radio, save configurations and make adjustments as needed. This is much more efficient than manually entering information through the radio's keypad, especially if you have multiple radios to configure.

A high-capacity battery is another accessory that can enhance your Baofeng radio experience. The standard battery is adequate for general use, but a larger battery pack can provide longer operating times, which is crucial during extended activities or emergencies. These batteries are designed to fit the radio just like the standard battery but offer more power, reducing the need for frequent recharging. Carrying an extra battery pack ensures that you always have a backup power source, keeping you connected when you need it most.

A desktop charger is a convenient accessory for keeping your Baofeng radio charged and ready to use. While the radio typically comes with a basic charger, a desktop charger can charge the radio more efficiently and often includes slots for charging additional batteries. This is particularly useful if you have multiple radios or extra batteries that need to be charged simultaneously. The desktop charger also provides a stable place to store your radio when it's not in use.

A sturdy carrying case can protect your Baofeng radio and its accessories. These cases are designed to fit the radio, antenna, battery and other small items, keeping everything organized and secure. A carrying case is especially useful when traveling or storing your radio for long periods. It protects the equipment from dust, moisture and physical damage, ensuring that your radio remains in good working condition.

For users who spend a lot of time in their vehicles, a car charger is a practical accessory. It allows you to charge your Baofeng radio directly from your vehicle's power outlet. This is especially useful for long trips or when you are on the road and need to keep your radio operational. Having a car charger ensures that your radio is always charged and ready to use, no matter where you are.

A handheld microphone with a speaker is another useful accessory for those who need to communicate clearly and effectively. These microphones often have additional features like noise-canceling technology, which improves audio quality by reducing background noise. They also provide the convenience of having the speaker closer to your ear, making it easier to hear messages in noisy environments.

A protective case or sleeve can help keep your radio in good condition. These cases are designed to fit snugly around the radio, providing protection from scratches, bumps and minor drops. Some cases are also water-resistant, offering additional protection in wet conditions. Using a protective case can extend the lifespan of your radio and keep it looking new.

A tactical pouch or holster is a great accessory for those who need to carry their radio while keeping their hands free. These pouches attach to belts, backpacks or other gear, providing easy access to the radio when needed. They are especially useful for hikers, campers and professionals who need to move around while staying connected.

By investing in these essential accessories, you can enhance the usability and functionality of your Baofeng radio, making it a more effective and convenient tool for communication in various situations.

CHAPTER 2

Mastering Basic Functions

Understanding Frequency: VHF vs. UHF

Understanding the difference between VHF (Very High Frequency) and UHF (Ultra High Frequency) is crucial when using Baofeng radios. Both frequency ranges have distinct characteristics that make them suitable for different applications. Knowing these differences will help you choose the right frequency for your needs.

VHF frequencies range from 30 MHz to 300 MHz. They are known for their ability to travel long distances and penetrate obstacles like trees and buildings better than UHF. This makes VHF ideal for outdoor use, such as in rural areas, open fields and forests. Because VHF waves are longer, they can bend around large obstacles and follow the curvature of the Earth. This is why VHF is commonly used in aviation, marine communication and by outdoor enthusiasts like hikers and campers.

One of the key advantages of VHF is its range. In open environments with minimal obstructions, VHF signals can travel very far, sometimes reaching up to several miles. This makes VHF an excellent choice for activities that require long-distance communication, such as boating and off-road adventures. Additionally, VHF frequencies are less crowded than UHF, reducing the chance of interference from other users.

However, VHF does have some limitations. Its performance can be significantly reduced in urban environments where buildings and other structures are common. VHF signals can struggle to penetrate dense materials like concrete and steel, leading to weaker signals and reduced range in cities. This is why VHF is less popular for urban use compared to UHF.

On the other hand, UHF frequencies range from 300 MHz to 3 GHz. UHF signals are better suited for short-range communication and can penetrate buildings, walls and other obstacles more effectively than VHF. This makes UHF ideal for use in urban areas, inside buildings, and in situations where you need reliable communication through various barriers. UHF is commonly used in public safety communications, business operations and by professional users who need dependable performance in dense environments.

UHF's ability to penetrate obstacles makes it a better choice for indoor use. For example, if you are using a Baofeng radio in a large building, warehouse, or factory, UHF frequencies will provide clearer and more reliable communication. UHF is also preferred for event coordination, security operations, and other activities that take place in areas with many obstructions.

Despite its advantages, UHF has a shorter range than VHF in open environments. UHF signals are more prone to attenuation, meaning they lose strength faster over distance and when passing through obstacles. This can be a disadvantage in outdoor settings where long-distance communication is required. Additionally, UHF frequencies are more crowded, which can lead to more interference from other users, especially in populated areas.

When choosing between VHF and UHF, consider the specific requirements of your situation. If you need long-range communication in open areas with minimal obstructions, VHF is likely the better choice. Its ability to travel farther and navigate around large obstacles makes it ideal for outdoor use. However, if you need reliable communication in urban environments, inside buildings, or in areas with many obstacles, UHF will perform better. Its ability to penetrate walls and other barriers ensures clearer communication in such conditions.

Many Baofeng radios are dual-band, meaning they can operate on both VHF and UHF frequencies. This versatility allows you to switch between bands depending on your needs. For instance, if you are hiking in the mountains, you might use VHF for its long-range capabilities. But if you are coordinating an event in a city, you can switch to UHF for better performance in an urban environment. This flexibility makes dual-band radios a valuable tool for various scenarios.

In summary, VHF and UHF frequencies each have their own strengths and weaknesses. VHF is best for long-distance communication in open areas with minimal obstructions, while UHF excels in short-range communication in environments with many obstacles. By understanding these differences and considering your specific needs, you can make an informed decision on which frequency to use with your Baofeng radio. This knowledge will help you maximize the performance and reliability of your radio in any situation.

Programming Channels Manually

Manually programming channels into your Baofeng radio is a straightforward process once you understand the steps. This allows you to set specific frequencies and channel names, customizing the radio to meet your communication needs. Here's a clear guide to help you through this process.

To start, ensure your Baofeng radio is turned on and fully charged. You'll be using the keypad and the display screen to enter information. Begin by switching to Frequency Mode, which allows you to input the desired frequency directly. You can do this by pressing the "VFO/MR" button, usually found on the front of the radio.

Once in Frequency Mode, you can enter the frequency you want to program. Use the keypad to type in the frequency directly. For example, if you want to set the frequency to 146.520 MHz, just press the buttons 1, 4, 6, 5, 2, and 0 in sequence. The display should show the frequency as you type it in. Make sure you enter the correct frequency, as this will be the basis for communication on this channel.

Next, you need to set the appropriate transmit (TX) and receive (RX) frequencies if you are using a repeater. Repeaters use two different frequencies for transmitting and receiving signals. To do this, first enter the receive frequency (RX) in Frequency Mode. After that, press the "MENU" button to access the menu options. Scroll through the menu using the arrow keys until you find the "OFFSET" option, which sets the frequency difference (offset) between the TX and RX frequencies.

Once you find the "OFFSET" option, press the "MENU" button again to select it. Use the keypad to enter the offset value, such as 0.600 for a 600 kHz offset. After entering the offset, press "MENU" again to confirm. Next, find the "SHIFT" or "SFT-D" option in the menu, which determines the direction of the offset (positive or negative). Set this to either "+" or "-" depending on the repeater's requirements, then confirm your selection by pressing "MENU."

After setting the frequencies, it's time to save the channel into the radio's memory. Press the "MENU" button and scroll to the "MEM-CH" (memory channel) option. Select it by pressing "MENU" again. Use the arrow keys to choose a memory slot where you want to save the channel. Each slot is numbered, and you can choose any available slot. Once you've selected a slot, press "MENU" to confirm and save the frequency to that channel.

To name the channel, you need to access the menu option for channel names. This might be labeled as "CH-NAME" or something similar. Enter this menu option, and use the keypad to type the name of the channel. The process of entering letters varies slightly depending on the model of your Baofeng radio, but generally, you will use the number keys to cycle through letters. For example, pressing the number 2 key repeatedly will cycle through A, B, C, and 2. Once you've entered the desired name, confirm it by pressing "MENU."

If your radio model supports it, you can also set additional parameters for the channel, such as CTCSS (Continuous Tone-Coded Squelch System) or DCS (Digital-Coded Squelch). These settings help filter out unwanted transmissions by only allowing signals with the correct tone or code to be heard. To set CTCSS or DCS, access the respective menu options (usually labeled "T-CTCS" for transmit CTCSS and "R-CTCS" for receive CTCSS) and select the desired tone or code using the keypad. Confirm your choices by pressing "MENU."

Finally, exit the menu by pressing the "EXIT" or "VFO/MR" button. Your channel is now programmed and saved in the radio's memory. To test it, switch to Memory Mode by pressing the "VFO/MR" button again, and use the arrow keys to navigate to the channel you just programmed. You should see the frequency and channel name displayed on the screen.

Repeat these steps for any additional channels you want to program. By understanding and following this process, you can customize your Baofeng radio to fit your specific communication needs, ensuring you have quick access to the frequencies and channels that are most important to you.

Using Repeater Channels for Extended Range

Repeater channels are specialized communication channels used to extend the range of your Baofeng radio. Repeaters are powerful radio systems that receive a signal on one frequency and then retransmit it on another frequency, thereby allowing communication over much greater distances than would be possible with simple point-to-point communication. Setting up repeater channels on your Baofeng radio involves programming both the receive (RX) and transmit (TX) frequencies correctly, along with any necessary access tones or codes.

To understand how repeaters work, think of them as relay stations. When you transmit a signal from your radio, the repeater picks it up and retransmits it on a different frequency. This retransmission is usually done from a high location like a hilltop, tall building, or dedicated communication tower, which helps the signal cover a larger area. This process effectively bypasses obstacles and extends the communication range significantly.

To set up a repeater channel on your Baofeng radio, start by identifying the necessary repeater frequencies and settings. You'll need the RX frequency (the frequency the repeater listens to) and the TX frequency (the frequency the repeater transmits on). These frequencies are often listed on repeater directories, which you can find online or through local radio clubs.

Once you have the necessary information, turn on your Baofeng radio and switch to Frequency Mode by pressing the "VFO/MR" button. This mode allows you to manually enter the frequencies. Begin by entering the RX frequency. Use the keypad to type in the frequency directly. For instance, if the RX frequency is 145.250 MHz, press the buttons 1, 4, 5, 2, 5, and 0 in sequence. The display should show the frequency as you type it in.

Next, you need to set the offset, which is the frequency difference between the RX and TX frequencies. This difference is known as the repeater shift or offset. Common offset values are ±600 kHz for VHF and ±5 MHz for UHF. To set the offset, press the "MENU" button to access the menu options, then scroll through the menu using the arrow keys until you find the "OFFSET" option.

Select the "OFFSET" option by pressing "MENU" again. Use the keypad to enter the offset value. For example, if the offset is 600 kHz, enter 0.600. After entering the offset, press "MENU" to confirm. Next, find the "SHIFT" or "SFT-D" option in the menu. This setting determines whether the offset is positive or negative, indicating whether the TX frequency is higher or lower than the RX frequency.

Select the "SHIFT" option and use the arrow keys to choose either "+" or "-" based on the repeater's specifications. Confirm your selection by pressing

"MENU." Now, your radio is set to use the correct RX and TX frequencies with the appropriate offset.

In addition to setting the frequencies and offset, some repeaters require an access tone, such as CTCSS (Continuous Tone-Coded Squelch System) or DCS (Digital-Coded Squelch), to allow access. These tones prevent unauthorized users from accessing the repeater and reduce interference. To set a CTCSS or DCS tone, press the "MENU" button and scroll through the options until you find "T-CTCS" for transmit CTCSS or "R-CTCS" for receive CTCSS.

Select the "T-CTCS" option by pressing "MENU" and then use the arrow keys to choose the correct tone frequency. After selecting the tone, press "MENU" to confirm. Repeat this process for the "R-CTCS" option if necessary. If the repeater uses DCS instead, look for "T-DCS" and "R-DCS" in the menu and follow the same steps to set the correct code.

Once all settings are configured, you need to save the repeater channel into the radio's memory. Press the "MENU" button and navigate to the "MEM-CH" (memory channel) option. Select it by pressing "MENU" again. Use the arrow keys to choose an available memory slot to save the channel. Each slot is numbered, and you can select any unused slot. Press "MENU" to confirm and save the frequency, offset, and tones to that channel.

To label the channel with a name, find the "CH-NAME" option in the menu. Enter this menu, and use the keypad to type the name. Each number key cycles through letters; for example, pressing the number 2 key repeatedly will go through A, B, C, and 2. Enter the desired name and confirm by pressing "MENU."

Now your repeater channel is programmed and saved. To test it, switch to Memory Mode by pressing the "VFO/MR" button, and use the arrow keys to navigate to the channel you just programmed. Ensure the display shows the correct frequency and name. Press the PTT (Push-To-Talk) button and speak into the radio. If everything is set up correctly, the repeater will receive your signal and retransmit it, extending your communication range.

Setting up repeater channels allows you to communicate over much greater distances, making your Baofeng radio more effective in a wider range of situations. Whether you are coordinating an event, participating in outdoor activities, or preparing for emergencies, understanding and using repeaters can significantly enhance your communication capabilities.

Scanning and Monitoring Multiple Channels

Using the scanning feature on your Baofeng radio allows you to monitor multiple channels simultaneously, making it easier to stay informed about activity across different frequencies. This can be particularly useful in various scenarios such as emergency preparedness, event coordination or general communication monitoring. Here's a comprehensive guide on how to use the scanning feature and tips for effective scanning.

First, ensure your Baofeng radio is turned on and fully charged. Scanning works in both Frequency Mode and Channel Mode, but it is typically more useful in Channel Mode where you have predefined channels stored in the radio's memory. To switch to Channel Mode, press the "VFO/MR" button.

In Channel Mode, you can start the scanning process by pressing and holding the "SCAN" button (usually labeled with an "S" or a similar symbol). The radio will begin scanning through the channels stored in its memory, pausing on any channel where it detects a signal. This allows you to listen in on active conversations or transmissions.

To effectively use the scanning feature, it's important to organize your channels logically. Group similar channels together, such as those used for specific events, emergency frequencies or general communication. This makes it easier to monitor relevant channels and quickly respond to any activity.

While scanning, the radio will pause on an active channel for a few seconds. If the signal continues, it will stay on that channel until the transmission ends or a set delay time expires. This delay time can usually be adjusted in the radio's settings menu. To change the delay time, press the "MENU" button and scroll through the options until you find the setting for "SCAN-D" (scan delay). Adjust the delay time using the arrow keys and confirm by pressing "MENU" again. A longer delay time allows you to listen to longer transmissions without the scan moving on too quickly.

If you hear something important and want to stop the scan on a specific channel, you can press the "SCAN" button again or the PTT (Push-To-Talk) button to manually stop the scan. This allows you to engage in communication or listen more closely to the ongoing transmission.

For effective scanning, consider using the "skip" feature to exclude certain channels from the scan list. This is useful if you have channels that are always busy with non-essential traffic or channels that you don't need to monitor. To skip a channel, first select the channel you want to exclude. Then press the "MENU" button and navigate to the "CH-SKIP" option. Use the arrow keys to select "ON" and press "MENU" to confirm. This will remove the channel from the scan list, making your scanning process more efficient.

Another useful feature is priority scanning, which allows you to monitor a priority channel more frequently than other channels. This is beneficial if you have a main channel that you need to monitor constantly while still scanning other channels. To set up priority scanning, you'll need to refer to your radio's manual, as the process can vary between different Baofeng models. Generally, you will set a priority channel in the settings menu and enable priority scanning. The radio will then check the priority channel at regular intervals while scanning other channels.

When scanning multiple channels, using dual-watch mode can be particularly helpful. Dual-watch mode allows the radio to monitor two channels simultaneously. To activate dual-watch mode, press the "MENU" button and navigate to the "TDR" option (dual-watch). Set this option to "ON" and confirm by pressing "MENU." With dual-watch mode enabled, you can set two different frequencies or channels to monitor, and the radio will switch between them as activity occurs.

For effective scanning, keep your radio's antenna in good condition and ensure it is suitable for the frequencies you are monitoring. A high-quality antenna can improve reception, making it easier to pick up weak signals and extend the range of your radio. If you are scanning in an area with a lot of interference, consider using a filter or adjusting the squelch settings to reduce background noise. The squelch setting controls the radio's sensitivity to weak signals. To adjust the squelch, press the "MENU" button and find the "SQL" option. Lower values make the radio more sensitive, while higher values reduce sensitivity to background noise.

It's also important to be aware of any legal restrictions or regulations regarding the use of certain frequencies. Ensure that you have the necessary permissions to monitor specific channels, especially if they are used by emergency services or other critical communications.

By following these steps and tips, you can effectively use the scanning feature on your Baofeng radio to monitor multiple channels simultaneously. This enhances your ability to stay informed and respond to communications as needed, making your radio a more versatile and powerful tool for various applications.

CHAPTER 3

Advanced Programming and Customization

Using Chirp Software for Programming

Chirp software is a powerful tool that simplifies the programming and customization of Baofeng radios. It allows users to easily manage channels, frequencies and other settings from their computer, making the process more efficient than manual programming. Here's a comprehensive guide on how to use Chirp software to program and customize your Baofeng radio.

To begin, you need to download and install Chirp software on your computer. Chirp is a free, open-source program available for Windows, macOS and Linux. Start by visiting the official

Chirp website (chirp.danplanet.com) to download the latest version. On the website, click on the download link for your operating system. Once the download is complete, open the installer file and follow the on-screen instructions to install the software. The installation process is straightforward, and you should be able to complete it within a few minutes.

After installing Chirp, you need a programming cable to connect your Baofeng radio to your computer. This cable typically has a USB connector on one end and a two-pin connector on the other end, which plugs into the radio. These cables are widely available online and often come with a Baofeng radio package. Connect the cable to your computer's USB port and plug the two-pin connector into the radio's speaker and microphone ports.

Before you can start programming, you may need to install the appropriate driver for the programming cable. Windows users can usually find the necessary drivers included with the cable or on the manufacturer's website. For macOS and Linux users, the drivers are often included with the operating system. Once the driver is installed, your computer should recognize the programming cable.

Next, turn on your Baofeng radio and open Chirp software on your computer. In Chirp, go to the "Radio" menu and select "Download From Radio." A dialog box will appear, prompting you to select the appropriate settings for your radio. Choose your radio's make and model from the drop-down menus, and select the correct COM port. The COM port is the connection point for the programming cable, and you can find it in your computer's device manager or system settings.

After selecting the correct settings, click "OK" to proceed. Chirp will begin downloading the current configuration from your radio. This process may take a few moments, and you'll see a progress bar indicating the status. Once the download is complete, Chirp will display a spreadsheet-like interface showing the current channels and settings on your radio.

You can now start customizing your radio's settings. To add a new channel, click on an empty row in the spreadsheet and enter the desired frequency, name and other parameters. For example, you can set the RX frequency, TX frequency (if using a repeater), channel name, CTCSS/DCS tones and other settings. Chirp allows you to easily copy and paste channel settings, making it simple to manage multiple channels.

If you have a list of frequencies you want to program, you can import them into Chirp. Go to the "File" menu and select "Import." Chirp supports importing from various formats, including CSV (comma-separated values) files. This feature is particularly useful if you have a large number of channels to program, as you can prepare the list in a spreadsheet application like Excel and then import it into Chirp.

In addition to adding and editing channels, Chirp also allows you to customize other radio settings. For example, you can adjust the power output, squelch levels and display settings. These options are accessible through the settings tabs in Chirp, and you can modify them to suit your preferences.

Once you have made all the desired changes, it's time to upload the new configuration to your radio. Go to the "Radio" menu and select "Upload To Radio." Chirp will prompt you to confirm the settings for your radio and the COM port. After confirming, click "OK" to begin the upload process. Chirp will transfer the new settings to your radio and you'll see a progress bar indicating the status. This process may take a few moments.

After the upload is complete, your Baofeng radio will have the new channels and settings you programmed using Chirp. It's a good idea to test the radio to ensure everything is working correctly. Tune to one of the newly programmed channels and check if the radio transmits and receives signals as expected.

Using Chirp software not only simplifies the programming process but also provides a backup of your radio's configuration. You can save your radio's settings as a Chirp file on your computer, allowing you to restore them easily if needed. To save your configuration, go to the "File" menu and select "Save As." Choose a location on your computer and save the file with a descriptive name.

If you need to reprogram your radio or update the settings in the future, you can open the saved Chirp file, make any necessary changes and upload the updated configuration to your radio. This feature is particularly useful for managing multiple radios or frequently changing frequencies.

In summary, Chirp software is a valuable tool for programming and customizing Baofeng radios. By following these steps, you can download, install and use Chirp to manage your radio's settings efficiently. This process not only saves time but also ensures that your radio is configured accurately for your communication needs.

Creating and Managing Channel Lists

Creating and managing channel lists on your Baofeng radio can be done using both manual methods and Chirp software. Properly organizing your channels ensures efficient communication and easy access to important frequencies. Here's a detailed guide on how to create and manage these lists effectively.

Manual Method

Start by turning on your Baofeng radio and switching to Frequency Mode by pressing the "VFO/MR" button. This mode allows you to manually enter the frequencies you wish to program. To input a new frequency, use the keypad to type it directly. For instance, if you want to program the frequency 145.600 MHz, press the buttons 1, 4, 5, 6, 0, and 0 in sequence. The frequency should appear on the display as you type.

Next, you need to set any additional parameters for the frequency, such as CTCSS or DCS tones, which help filter out unwanted transmissions. To do this, press the "MENU" button to access the menu options. Scroll through the menu using the arrow keys until you find the options for "T-CTCS" (transmit CTCSS) and "R-CTCS" (receive CTCSS). Select each option by pressing "MENU" again, and then use the arrow keys to choose the desired tone. Confirm each selection by pressing "MENU."

After setting the frequency and tones, save the channel to your radio's memory. Press "MENU" and scroll to the "MEM-CH" (memory channel) option. Select it by pressing "MENU" and use the arrow keys to choose an available memory slot. Press "MENU" to confirm and save the channel. Repeat this process for each frequency you want to program, ensuring each channel is saved to a unique memory slot.

To manage your channel list manually, it's useful to keep a written record of each programmed channel, including its frequency, name and any additional parameters. This record helps you track your channels and make changes as needed. Organize your channels by grouping similar ones together, such as all emergency frequencies or all local repeaters, to make navigation easier.

Using Chirp Software

Using Chirp software greatly simplifies creating and managing channel lists. Start by connecting your Baofeng radio to your computer with a programming cable and ensuring Chirp is installed. Open Chirp and download the current configuration from your radio by selecting "Download From

Radio" in the "Radio" menu. Choose your radio's make and model and the correct COM port, then click "OK."

Chirp will display your radio's current channel list in a spreadsheet-like interface. To create a new channel, click on an empty row and enter the frequency, name, and any additional settings like CTCSS/DCS tones. Chirp allows you to copy and paste settings, making it easy to manage multiple channels. For example, if you have several frequencies with the same tone settings, you can quickly duplicate this information.

You can also import a list of frequencies from a file. Go to the "File" menu and select "Import," then choose a CSV file or other supported formats. This feature is especially useful if you have a large number of channels to program. Prepare your list in a spreadsheet application like Excel, then import it into Chirp to save time.

Organize your channels in Chirp by grouping them logically. For instance, place all emergency channels in a consecutive block, followed by local repeaters and then personal or recreational frequencies. This organization helps you quickly find and access the channels you need.

After organizing and entering all desired channels, upload the new configuration to your radio by selecting "Upload To Radio" in the "Radio" menu. Confirm the settings and COM port, then click "OK" to start the upload. Chirp will transfer the updated channel list to your radio, and you'll see a progress bar indicating the status.

To keep your channel lists organized, save the Chirp file with a descriptive name. This allows you to easily update and reprogram your radio in the future. Go to the "File" menu and select "Save As," then choose a location on your computer and enter a name for the file.

Tips for Organization and Efficiency

1. Categorize Channels: Group similar channels together, such as emergency services, local repeater and personal channels. This categorization helps you quickly find the channels you need in different situations.

2. Label Clearly: Use descriptive names for each channel to make identification easy. Instead of generic names, use labels like "Local Repeater," "Fire Dept," or "Camping Channel."

3. Backup Regularly: Save your channel list configurations regularly in Chirp. This practice ensures you can easily restore your settings if you need to reset your radio or transfer them to a new device.

4. Use Aliases: For commonly used frequencies, consider setting up aliases or shortcut names. This makes it faster to switch to important channels without remembering the exact frequency numbers.

5. Test and Adjust: After programming your channels, test them to ensure they work as expected. Make any necessary adjustments in Chirp and upload the updated configuration to your radio.

6. Frequency Resources: Use online resources and local radio clubs to find recommended frequencies for your area. These sources can provide valuable information on active repeaters, emergency channels and other useful frequencies.

7. Regular Updates: Keep your channel lists updated by periodically reviewing and adding new frequencies. Remove any channels that are no longer needed to keep your list efficient and relevant.

By following these steps and tips, you can effectively create and manage channel lists on your Baofeng radio using both manual methods and Chirp software. This organization enhances your communication capabilities, ensuring you can quickly and efficiently access the channels you need in various situations.

Setting Up CTCSS/DCS Codes for Privacy

CTCSS (Continuous Tone-Coded Squelch System) and DCS (Digital-Coded Squelch) codes are used to filter out unwanted transmissions on your Baofeng radio, enabling more private and clear communication. These codes don't encrypt your communication but reduce interference by ensuring that only radios set to the same tone or code can hear each other. Here's how to understand and set up CTCSS and DCS codes on your Baofeng radio.

CTCSS codes are analog tones that are transmitted along with your voice signal. When you set a CTCSS code on your radio, it will only open the squelch (allow you to hear) if it receives the same CTCSS tone from another radio. This helps reduce noise and interference from other users on the same frequency. There are 50 standard CTCSS tones, each identified by a specific frequency.

DCS codes, on the other hand, are digital and provide a similar function. Instead of a continuous tone, DCS sends a digital code. DCS offers more codes than CTCSS, typically 104, providing a higher level of specificity and privacy. Like CTCSS, DCS codes need to match on both transmitting and receiving radios to allow communication.

To set up CTCSS or DCS codes on your Baofeng radio, follow these steps:

1. Power On and Enter Frequency Mode: Turn on your Baofeng radio and switch to Frequency Mode by pressing the "VFO/MR" button. This mode allows you to enter the frequency you want to use and set up CTCSS/DCS codes.

2. Select the Desired Frequency: Use the keypad to enter the frequency you want to program. For example, if your desired frequency is 145.500 MHz, type in 1, 4, 5, 5, 0, 0.

3. Access the Menu: Press the "MENU" button to enter the menu options. The menu contains various settings you can adjust, including CTCSS and DCS codes.

4. Set CTCSS Code: Scroll through the menu using the arrow keys until you find the "T-CTCS" option, which stands for Transmit CTCSS. Press "MENU" again to select it. Use the arrow keys to choose the desired CTCSS tone from the list. Each tone corresponds to a specific frequency, such as 67.0 Hz, 71.9 Hz and so on. Once you've selected the desired tone, press "MENU" to confirm.

Next, set the Receive CTCSS code by finding the "R-CTCS" option in the menu. Select it by pressing "MENU" and use the arrow keys to choose the same CTCSS tone you set for transmitting. Confirm by pressing "MENU" again. Setting both transmit and receive CTCSS codes ensures your radio only communicates with others using the same tone.

5. Set DCS Code: If you prefer to use DCS codes, follow a similar process. Find the "T-DCS" option in the menu for Transmit DCS and select it by pressing "MENU." Use the arrow keys to choose the desired DCS code, such as D023N, D025N etc. Confirm your choice by pressing "MENU."

Then, set the Receive DCS code by finding the "R-DCS" option. Select it and use the arrow keys to choose the same DCS code. Confirm by pressing "MENU." As with CTCSS, setting matching transmit and receive DCS codes ensures your radio filters out unwanted signals.

6. Save the Settings: After setting the CTCSS or DCS codes, save the frequency and codes to a memory channel. Press "MENU" and scroll to the

"MEM-CH" option. Select it, choose an available memory slot using the arrow keys and press "MENU" to save.

7. Test the Setup: Once you've set up and saved the codes, test the communication with another radio programmed to the same frequency and codes. Ensure that you can only hear transmissions when both radios use matching CTCSS or DCS codes.

Tips for Effective Use

Consistency: Ensure all radios in your group use the same CTCSS or DCS codes. Inconsistent settings will prevent radios from communicating with each other.

Avoid Common Tones: Choose less common CTCSS or DCS codes to minimize interference from other users who might be on the same frequency but using standard tones.

Label Channels: Clearly label the channels on your radio with the corresponding CTCSS or DCS codes. This helps avoid confusion and ensures you select the correct channel during communication.

Monitor Channels: Occasionally switch to an open frequency without CTCSS or DCS codes to monitor for important transmissions that might not use these filters.

Backup Settings: Keep a written record or backup file of your programmed frequencies and codes. This is useful for reprogramming or sharing settings with new group members.

By understanding and setting up CTCSS and DCS codes on your Baofeng radio, you can significantly enhance the privacy and clarity of your communications. These codes help filter out unwanted noise and ensure that you only hear transmissions intended for your group. With careful setup and management, CTCSS and DCS codes make your radio communications more efficient and effective.

Configuring Dual Watch and Dual Standby Modes

Baofeng radios come equipped with dual watch and dual standby modes, which are useful features for monitoring multiple frequencies simultaneously. Understanding and setting up these modes can significantly enhance your communication capabilities. Here's a comprehensive guide on these features and how to configure them on your Baofeng radio.

Dual Watch Mode

Dual watch mode allows you to monitor two frequencies at the same time. This feature is particularly useful if you need to keep an ear on a primary channel while also staying aware of communications on a secondary frequency. The radio will primarily stay on the main frequency but will switch to the secondary frequency if there is any activity.

To set up dual watch mode:

1. Power On the Radio: Turn on your Baofeng radio by rotating the volume knob clockwise. You should hear a beep indicating the radio is on.

2. Enter Frequency Mode: Press the "VFO/MR" button to switch to Frequency Mode if you are not already in this mode. This allows you to manually enter the frequencies you want to monitor.

3. Select the First Frequency: Use the keypad to enter the primary frequency you want to monitor. For example, if your primary frequency is 145.500 MHz, type in 1, 4, 5, 5, 0, 0. Ensure this frequency is displayed on the top line of the screen (A band).

4. Select the Second Frequency: Press the "A/B" button to switch to the bottom line of the screen (B band). Use the keypad to enter the secondary frequency you want to monitor, such as 146.520 MHz. Type in 1, 4, 6, 5, 2, 0.

5. Activate Dual Watch Mode: Press the "MENU" button to access the menu options. Scroll through the menu using the arrow keys until you find the "TDR" (Dual Watch/Dual Reception) option. Press "MENU" to select it. Use the arrow keys to choose "ON," and press "MENU" again to confirm.

6. Save the Settings: Exit the menu by pressing the "EXIT" button. Your radio is now set to dual watch mode and will monitor both frequencies. The display will show both frequencies, and the radio will switch to the active frequency if there is any transmission.

Dual Standby Mode

Dual standby mode is similar to dual watch mode, but it allows the radio to listen to both frequencies and switch automatically to the one that is active. This means you can effectively monitor two channels and respond to communications on either without manually switching between them.

To set up dual standby mode:

1. Power On the Radio: Ensure your Baofeng radio is turned on.

2. Enter Frequency Mode: Press the "VFO/MR" button to switch to Frequency Mode.

3. Select the First Frequency: Enter the primary frequency on the top line of the screen (A band).

4. Select the Second Frequency: Switch to the bottom line of the screen (B band) and enter the secondary frequency.

5. Activate Dual Standby Mode: This mode is automatically engaged when you set dual watch mode. The radio will remain on the last active frequency until activity is detected on the other frequency, at which point it will switch to that frequency.

Configuring Additional Settings for Both Modes

1. Priority Channel: If you want one of the frequencies to be prioritized over the other, you can set it as the priority channel. Press the "MENU" button and scroll to the "PRI" option. Select it, choose "ON," and confirm with "MENU." The radio will periodically check the priority channel for activity and switch to it if a transmission is detected.

2. Setting Tones: You can also set CTCSS or DCS codes for each frequency to filter out unwanted signals. Enter the menu and find the "T-CTCS" or "R-CTCS" options for CTCSS tones or "T-DCS" and "R-DCS" for DCS codes. Set these codes as needed for each frequency.

3. Volume Balancing: Ensure that the volume levels for both frequencies are appropriately set.

You can adjust the volume by rotating the volume knob. Make sure both frequencies are audible enough to catch any communication.

Tips for Using Dual Watch and Dual Standby Modes

Monitor Important Channels: Use these modes to keep track of emergency channels or other important frequencies while continuing your regular communication.

Battery Management: Dual watch and dual standby modes can drain the battery faster because the radio is constantly monitoring two frequencies. Keep spare batteries handy or use a battery saver mode if available.

Clear Communication: When using dual watch or dual standby, speak clearly and listen carefully to avoid missing transmissions. The radio may switch between frequencies quickly and clear communication helps ensure no important messages are missed.

Test Settings: After setting up these modes, test the radio to ensure it switches correctly between frequencies and that you can hear transmissions on both. This ensures that your configuration is correct and functional.

Regular Updates: Periodically review and update the frequencies you monitor to ensure they remain relevant. Frequencies in use can change over time and keeping your channel list current ensures effective communication.

By understanding and utilizing dual watch and dual standby modes on your Baofeng radio, you can significantly enhance your communication capabilities. These features allow you to monitor multiple channels, ensuring you stay informed and connected in various situations. Proper setup and management of these modes ensure you make the most of your Baofeng radio's functionality.

CHAPTER 4

Practical Applications for Everyday Use

Communicating in Urban Environments

Effective radio communication in urban environments requires strategies that account for obstacles like buildings, interference from other electronic devices and varying terrain. Urban areas present unique challenges, but with the right techniques and tools, you can maintain clear and reliable communication using your Baofeng radio.

One of the primary obstacles in urban areas is the presence of buildings, which can block or reflect radio signals. To overcome this, choose higher frequencies for your communications. VHF (Very High Frequency) signals, while useful in open areas, can struggle with obstacles. UHF (Ultra High Frequency) signals, on the other hand, are better at penetrating buildings and navigating through urban landscapes. Therefore, using UHF frequencies can improve your communication clarity in cities.

Positioning is another crucial factor. When using your Baofeng radio, try to position yourself in elevated locations whenever possible. Higher ground or rooftops can provide a clearer line of sight for your radio signals, reducing the impact of buildings and other structures. If you are inside a building, move close to a window or an open area to enhance signal reception and transmission.

Antennas play a significant role in improving communication quality. The stock antenna that comes with most Baofeng radios is often not the most efficient for urban environments. Upgrading to a higher-gain antenna can significantly enhance your radio's performance. A high-gain antenna can extend the range and clarity of your transmissions by focusing the signal more effectively, which is particularly useful in areas with many obstacles.

Interference from other electronic devices is another common issue in urban settings. Devices like Wi-Fi routers, cell towers and even other radios can cause signal interference. To minimize this, use CTCSS (Continuous Tone-Coded Squelch System) or DCS (Digital-Coded Squelch) codes. These codes help filter out unwanted signals and ensure that your radio only responds to transmissions on the same frequency with the same tone or code, reducing the impact of interference.

Repeater stations are a valuable resource in urban areas. Repeaters receive your radio signal and retransmit it at a higher power, effectively extending your communication range. Many cities have numerous repeaters set up by amateur radio clubs or emergency services. Find out the locations and frequencies of local repeaters and program them into your Baofeng radio. Using repeaters can greatly enhance your ability to communicate over longer distances and through obstacles.

Regularly monitoring and adjusting your frequency can also help maintain clear communication. Urban environments are dynamic, with various signals constantly changing. If you experience interference or poor signal quality, try switching to a different frequency. Keeping a list of alternate frequencies and repeaters can provide options when your primary frequency becomes unusable.

Effective communication also depends on proper radio etiquette and clear, concise messaging. In urban environments where many people might be using radios, it's important to avoid long transmissions that can tie up frequencies. Speak clearly and directly, also ensure that your messages are brief but informative. Using standard communication protocols, such as identifying yourself and your location at the beginning of each transmission, can help reduce confusion and ensure your messages are understood.

Environmental noise is another consideration. Urban areas are often noisy, with sounds from traffic, construction and crowds. Use an external microphone or earpiece to improve audio quality. An external microphone can help capture your voice more clearly, while an earpiece ensures you can hear incoming transmissions despite background noise. These accessories can be particularly useful when communicating in noisy environments or while moving.

Battery life is crucial for effective communication. Urban environments may require longer transmission times and higher power settings, which can drain your battery faster. Carry spare batteries or a portable charger to ensure you don't run out of power when you need it most. Regularly check your battery status and be prepared with backups to maintain uninterrupted communication.

Planning and preparation are key to successful urban communication. Before heading into an urban area, plan your communication strategy. Identify key locations, such as high points or areas with known good reception and plan your routes accordingly. Share your communication plan with your team, ensuring everyone knows which frequencies to use and any backup plans if primary communications fail.

Safety is always a priority. In urban environments, ensure your radio is set up for emergency use. Program emergency channels and local emergency services frequencies into your radio. Make sure you and your team know how to quickly switch to these channels if needed. Having a clear emergency communication plan can be crucial in situations where quick and reliable communication is essential.

Using your Baofeng radio effectively in urban environments involves a combination of technical adjustments and practical strategies. By choosing the right frequencies, upgrading your antenna, using repeaters, minimizing interference and following proper communication protocols, you can maintain clear and reliable communication even in the challenging conditions of a city. With preparation and the right tools, your Baofeng radio can be a valuable asset for staying connected in any urban setting.

Using Baofeng Radios for Outdoor Adventures

Baofeng radios are invaluable tools for outdoor adventures like hiking, camping, and boating. They provide reliable communication in remote areas where cell service may be unavailable, ensuring safety and coordination among your group. Understanding how to effectively use these radios in outdoor settings can enhance your experience and keep everyone connected.

When preparing for an outdoor adventure, one of the first steps is to ensure your Baofeng radio is properly charged and you have spare batteries. Outdoor activities can be unpredictable and having extra power sources is crucial to maintaining communication. Consider investing in a solar charger or a portable battery pack to recharge your radio in the field.

Choosing the right frequencies is essential for effective communication. In remote areas, VHF (Very High Frequency) signals often work better because they travel farther in open spaces and over water. For hiking and camping in forests or mountainous terrain, UHF (Ultra High Frequency) may be more effective as it can better penetrate dense foliage and obstacles. Pre-program your radios with a range of frequencies, including local emergency channels and common frequencies used by outdoor enthusiasts.

A key feature of Baofeng radios for outdoor use is the ability to scan channels. This allows you to monitor multiple frequencies and find active channels quickly. Scanning is especially useful when boating or hiking in areas where other groups may also be using radios. It helps you stay aware of nearby activities and communicate with others if necessary.

Understanding and using repeaters can greatly enhance your communication range. Repeaters are devices that receive your signal and retransmit it at a higher power, extending the reach of your radio. Before heading out, research the locations and frequencies of any repeaters in the area. Many outdoor regions have repeaters set up by local amateur radio clubs or emergency services. Programming these into your radio can provide a significant communication advantage in remote areas.

Effective antenna use is critical for maximizing your radio's range. The standard antenna that comes with Baofeng radios may not always provide the best performance in rugged terrain. Upgrading to a higher-gain antenna can improve signal transmission and reception. Additionally, consider carrying a telescopic or flexible antenna that can be adjusted for better performance in varying conditions.

When using Baofeng radios for hiking, consider the terrain and your location. Higher elevations generally offer better signal range. If possible, try to communicate from hilltops or open areas rather than valleys or heavily forested regions. If you're separated from your group, moving to a higher location can improve your chances of re-establishing contact.

For camping, establish a communication plan with your group before setting up camp. Designate a common frequency and ensure everyone knows how to operate their radios. Regular check-ins help keep everyone informed about their locations and activities. In larger campsites, use the radios to coordinate group activities, share important information or call for help if needed.

Boating presents unique challenges due to the expansive nature of water and potential interference from the environment. For boating activities, VHF frequencies are typically more effective. Ensure your radio is waterproof or at least water-resistant, as exposure to water is a common risk. Use a buoyant radio case or attach a flotation device to your radio to prevent it from sinking if it falls overboard.

Weather conditions can significantly impact radio communication. In outdoor settings, be aware of weather forecasts and plan accordingly. Rain, fog and other weather conditions can affect signal strength and clarity. Having a weatherproof radio or protective case can help maintain communication in adverse conditions.

Clear and concise communication is vital in outdoor adventures. Use standard radio protocols, such as identifying yourself and your location at the beginning of each transmission. Keep messages brief and to the point to avoid tying up the channel and ensure that important information is conveyed efficiently. In emergency situations, use universally recognized distress signals and protocols to call for help.

Safety should always be a priority when using radios in outdoor activities. Program local emergency frequencies and the frequencies of any park rangers or rescue services into your radio. Make sure everyone in your group knows how to switch to these frequencies and call for help if necessary. Regularly check the functionality of your radio, including battery levels and signal clarity, to ensure it's ready for use in an emergency.

Training and practice are essential for effective radio use. Before embarking on your outdoor adventure, take time to familiarize yourself with your Baofeng radio's functions and features. Practice using the radio with your group, including how to change frequencies, use the scanning feature, and switch to emergency channels. The more comfortable you are with your radio, the more effectively you'll be able to use it in the field.

Baofeng radios can significantly enhance the safety and enjoyment of your outdoor adventures by providing reliable communication in remote areas. Proper preparation, including charging and maintaining your radio, choosing appropriate frequencies, understanding and using repeaters, upgrading antennas, and practicing clear communication protocols, is crucial. With these strategies, you can ensure that your Baofeng radio is an effective tool for staying connected during hiking, camping, and boating activities, keeping you and your group safe and informed.

Coordination in Events

Using Baofeng radios to coordinate activities at large events like festivals, sports events and community gatherings can greatly enhance organization, safety and efficiency. These radios offer reliable, instant communication that helps keep everyone on the same page, whether you're managing a team of volunteers, ensuring crowd control or responding to emergencies.

For festivals, communication is crucial for managing various aspects such as stage performances, vendor coordination, security and medical emergencies. Assigning specific frequencies for different teams can help streamline communication. For instance, you might have one channel for stage managers, another for security personnel and a third for medical teams. This prevents channel congestion and ensures that each team can communicate effectively without interference.

When setting up communication for a festival, it's important to conduct a pre-event briefing with all radio users. During this briefing, distribute radios, explain the designated channels for each team and ensure everyone knows how to operate the radios. Providing a quick tutorial on how to switch channels, adjust volume and use emergency features can prevent confusion during the event.

Sports events also benefit greatly from the use of Baofeng radios. Coordinating activities like team logistics, spectator management and emergency response requires efficient communication. Coaches, referees, event staff and security personnel can use radios to stay in constant contact. For example, if a coach needs to make last-minute adjustments or substitutions, they can quickly communicate with team members or assistants. Similarly, event staff can manage the flow of spectators, direct people to seating areas and handle any disruptions that occur.

Effective radio use in sports events also involves strategic placement of key personnel. Positioning individuals with radios at critical points such as entrances, exits and high-traffic areas ensures swift communication and response. This setup helps in monitoring crowd movement and addressing any issues promptly, thereby enhancing the overall experience for participants and spectators.

Community activities, such as parades, fairs and neighborhood cleanups, also benefit from using Baofeng radios. Organizers can maintain contact with volunteers, coordinate activities, and address any issues that arise. For example, during a neighborhood cleanup, team leaders can use radios to direct volunteers to specific areas that need attention, manage supplies and coordinate pick-up points for collected trash.

Safety is a primary concern at large events and Baofeng radios play a vital role in emergency communication. Establishing a clear protocol for emergencies is essential. Designate a specific channel for emergency use and ensure all radio users know how to switch to it quickly. In case of a medical emergency, security threat or lost child, immediate communication can facilitate a rapid response. Event organizers should also conduct regular checks to ensure all radios are functioning properly and have sufficient battery life.

To maximize the effectiveness of Baofeng radios, it's important to use accessories that enhance communication. External microphones and earpieces can improve audio clarity in noisy environments, such as concerts or sports events. These accessories allow users to hear and transmit messages clearly, even amidst loud background noise. Additionally, using high-gain antennas can extend the range of the radios, ensuring better coverage across large venues.

Organizers should also consider the layout of the event when planning radio communication. For instance, in a festival spread over a large area, placing relay stations or repeaters can help extend the range of the radios. This ensures that communication remains clear even if team members are far apart or if there are obstacles like buildings or stages.

Regular check-ins and updates during the event are crucial for maintaining effective communication. Scheduling periodic check-ins helps ensure that all teams are functioning smoothly and that any issues are promptly addressed. These check-ins can be brief but should cover essential updates, such as changes in schedule, potential safety concerns and coordination of tasks.

Clear and concise communication protocols are important to avoid misunderstandings and ensure efficient use of the radio channels. Encourage users to keep messages short and to the point. Standard phrases and codes can be useful for common situations, reducing the need for lengthy explanations. For example, using simple codes for different types of incidents (e.g., "Code Red" for medical emergencies) can streamline communication and improve response times.

Training is essential for effective radio use. Providing comprehensive training sessions before the event helps users become familiar with the radio's features and functions. Practical exercises, such as role-playing different scenarios, can help users practice switching channels, making emergency calls and using accessories. The more comfortable users are with their radios, the more effectively they will communicate during the event.

Baofeng radios are powerful tools for coordinating activities at large events like festivals, sports events and community gatherings. By assigning specific channels to different teams, conducting pre-event briefings and using appropriate accessories, organizers can enhance communication and ensure smooth operation. Regular check-ins, clear communication protocols and thorough training further contribute to effective radio use. With these strategies, Baofeng radios can help create a safer, more organized and enjoyable experience for everyone involved in the event.

Enhancing Safety and Security

Baofeng radios are valuable tools for enhancing personal and community safety, offering reliable and immediate communication that can make a significant difference in emergency situations. Their role in neighborhood watch programs and personal protection is particularly noteworthy, providing a direct line of contact between community members and authorities.

Neighborhood watch programs rely on strong communication networks to monitor and report suspicious activities effectively. Baofeng radios facilitate this by enabling real-time communication among residents. When a suspicious activity is observed, members can quickly alert each other and coordinate a response. This rapid communication can deter potential criminals and ensure that incidents are reported to the police promptly.

Setting up a neighborhood watch program with Baofeng radios involves organizing and training community members. Start by assigning radios to key individuals in different areas of the neighborhood. Establish designated channels for routine communication and emergencies. It's crucial to conduct regular training sessions so everyone knows how to operate the radios, switch channels and use emergency features.

Effective use of Baofeng radios in neighborhood watch programs also involves creating a clear protocol for different situations. For instance, if a member spots a suspicious person, they can use a specific code or phrase to alert others without alarming the suspect. This discreet communication helps in gathering more information and planning a coordinated response without escalating the situation.

Personal security is another area where Baofeng radios shine. Whether you are at home, traveling, or engaging in outdoor activities, having a Baofeng radio can provide an extra layer of safety. For instance, if you are hiking alone in a remote area, carrying a Baofeng radio allows you to stay in contact with family or friends. In case of an emergency, you can quickly call for help, providing your exact location and details of the situation.

For personal security, it's important to familiarize yourself with local emergency frequencies and program them into your radio. This ensures you can reach emergency services quickly if needed. Additionally, using accessories like earpieces can help you communicate discreetly, which is useful in situations where you don't want to draw attention to yourself.

In family settings, Baofeng radios can be used to keep track of children or elderly family members. For example, if your children are playing outside or you are at a large event, providing them with radios ensures they can easily contact you if they need help. This gives peace of mind and enhances safety by maintaining a direct line of communication.

Neighborhood watch programs benefit from the range and clarity of Baofeng radios, which can cover large areas and penetrate buildings. Organizing regular check-ins and patrols using these radios helps maintain vigilance. Members can coordinate patrol schedules, share updates on their observations and quickly mobilize in response to incidents.

In addition to monitoring and reporting, Baofeng radios can facilitate community engagement and proactive safety measures. For instance, members can use radios to organize neighborhood clean-ups, community meetings and safety drills. These activities not only improve the neighborhood but also strengthen the sense of community and collective responsibility for safety.

Baofeng radios also play a crucial role in disaster preparedness and response. In the event of natural disasters like earthquakes, floods or storms, conventional communication networks often fail. Baofeng radios provide a reliable alternative, enabling residents to communicate with each other and with emergency services. Organizing community drills and training sessions on using radios during disasters can significantly enhance preparedness and response capabilities.

Privacy and security in communication are important considerations. Using CTCSS (Continuous Tone-Coded Squelch System) or DCS (Digital-Coded Squelch) codes on your Baofeng radio can help reduce interference and ensure that only your group can hear the transmissions. This is particularly useful in densely populated areas where many people might be using radios.

For personal protection, carrying a Baofeng radio when traveling alone, especially in unfamiliar or remote areas, can be a lifesaver. If you encounter trouble or feel threatened, you can use the radio to contact friends, family or emergency services. It's also advisable to keep your radio within easy reach and ensure it's fully charged before heading out.

Neighborhood watch programs can also collaborate with local law enforcement. Sharing information about watch activities and integrating Baofeng radio communication with police frequencies (where legally allowed) can enhance coordination and response times. Law enforcement can provide guidance on effective communication practices and respond more swiftly to incidents reported via neighborhood watch channels.

In community events, Baofeng radios help manage crowd control and ensure safety. Organizers can use radios to communicate with volunteers, coordinate activities and respond to emergencies. This level of coordination is essential for preventing incidents and handling them efficiently if they occur.

Baofeng radios significantly enhance personal and community safety through reliable, instant communication. In neighborhood watch programs, they enable coordinated monitoring and response to suspicious activities, strengthening community vigilance. For personal protection, they provide an essential communication link in emergencies, whether at home, traveling or outdoors. By integrating Baofeng radios into safety protocols, conducting regular training and collaborating with local authorities, communities can build robust safety networks that protect residents and foster a secure environment.

CHAPTER 5

Emergency Preparedness and Disaster Communication

The Role of Radios in Emergency Situations

Two-way radios play a critical role in emergency situations by providing reliable communication when other systems fail. During disasters, traditional communication networks like phone lines and cell towers can become overwhelmed or damaged, making it difficult to call for help or coordinate responses. Two-way radios, such as Baofeng radios, offer a robust and independent communication method that can be a lifeline in these scenarios.

One key advantage of two-way radios is their ability to function without relying on external infrastructure. Unlike cell phones, which depend on cell towers, two-way radios operate on dedicated frequencies and can communicate directly with each other. This makes them particularly valuable in natural disasters like earthquakes, hurricanes, or wildfires, where infrastructure may be compromised. In such events, two-way radios enable first responders, emergency services and community members to maintain contact and coordinate rescue efforts.

For instance, during an earthquake, phone lines may be down and cell networks overloaded, making it difficult to reach emergency services. Two-way radios allow residents to communicate with each other and with emergency personnel, providing updates on their status and receiving instructions on how to stay safe. Community members can use radios to report their locations, share information about hazards and request assistance, ensuring that help reaches those in need more efficiently.

In hurricane scenarios, where widespread power outages and flooding are common, two-way radios are indispensable for both emergency responders and the affected population. Emergency teams use radios to coordinate rescue operations, direct resources and communicate with shelters. Residents can use them to stay informed about evacuation orders, find safe routes and receive real-time updates on the storm's progress. Radios can also facilitate communication between neighbors, allowing them to assist each other and share vital resources.

Wildfires present another situation where two-way radios are essential. Fast-moving fires can quickly disrupt communication networks, making it difficult for emergency services to coordinate their efforts. Firefighters use radios to communicate across the fire line, share information about fire behavior and manage evacuations. Residents in fire-prone areas often have radios on hand to receive evacuation alerts and updates on fire containment efforts. By maintaining clear and constant communication, radios help save lives and property during these fast-paced emergencies.

In addition to natural disasters, two-way radios are crucial during man-made emergencies, such as industrial accidents or terrorist attacks. For example, in the event of a chemical spill at an industrial plant, workers and emergency responders need to communicate quickly to contain the hazard and evacuate the area. Radios allow for immediate, clear communication, enabling swift action that can prevent further harm. Similarly, in the aftermath of a terrorist attack, radios ensure that emergency services can coordinate their responses, manage the scene and provide accurate information to the public.

Two-way radios are also vital for community emergency preparedness plans. Neighborhood watch groups, community emergency response teams (CERTs) and local volunteers can use radios to organize and conduct drills, ensuring everyone knows how to use the equipment and follow emergency protocols. In an actual emergency, these groups can quickly mobilize, using radios to maintain communication and coordinate their efforts. This community-level preparedness enhances overall resilience and can significantly reduce the impact of disasters.

Emergency kits often include two-way radios as a standard component, underscoring their importance in preparedness. Families are encouraged to keep radios in their emergency supplies, along with extra batteries and a list of programmed frequencies. Knowing how to use the radios and which channels to use can make a significant difference during an emergency. Parents can teach their children how to operate the radios, ensuring that everyone in the household is prepared to communicate if separated.

Another critical aspect of two-way radios in emergencies is their role in search and rescue operations. After a disaster, search and rescue teams use radios to coordinate their efforts, share information about areas that have been searched, and report findings. This communication is essential for efficient and effective operations, helping to locate and rescue survivors as quickly as possible. Radios also enable these teams to stay in contact with command centers, ensuring that they receive timely updates and instructions.

For large-scale emergencies that affect entire regions, such as a nationwide blackout or a major terrorist attack, two-way radios provide a means for authorities to disseminate information and coordinate a response. Government agencies and emergency services can use dedicated radio frequencies to communicate with each other and with the public, ensuring that accurate and timely information is available even when other communication channels are down.

Radios also facilitate communication between different organizations involved in emergency response. Police, fire departments, medical team and utility companies often need to work together during a disaster. Radios allow these diverse groups to communicate effectively, share resources and synchronize their efforts, leading to a more organized and efficient response.

In conclusion, two-way radios are indispensable in emergency situations for maintaining communication when traditional systems fail. Their ability to operate independently of external infrastructure, provide reliable communication over various distances and support coordination among diverse groups makes them a crucial tool in disaster response and preparedness. Whether during natural disasters, industrial accidents or large-scale emergencies, two-way radios ensure that emergency services and community members can stay connected, share critical information and respond effectively, ultimately saving lives and reducing the impact of these crises.

Setting Up an Emergency Communication Plan

Creating an emergency communication plan using Baofeng radios involves several key steps to ensure that you and your family or community can stay connected during a crisis. The process includes selecting appropriate equipment, programming the radios, establishing communication protocols and conducting regular drills. By following these steps, you can create a reliable and effective plan that enhances safety and coordination during emergencies.

The first step in setting up an emergency communication plan is to choose the right equipment. Baofeng radios are a popular choice due to their affordability, versatility and user-friendly features. Ensure that each family member or key community participant has a radio. It's important to consider additional accessories, such as extra batteries, chargers, earpieces and high-gain antennas, to enhance the radios' performance and ensure they are ready for use when needed.

Programming the radios is a crucial part of the setup. Begin by identifying the frequencies that will be used for communication. These can include local emergency frequencies, family or community channels and specific frequencies for different teams or groups. Baofeng radios allow you to manually program these frequencies or use software like Chirp to simplify the process. Make sure all radios are programmed with the same channels to ensure seamless communication.

Once the radios are programmed, establish clear communication protocols. Decide on a primary channel for general communication and additional channels for specific purposes, such as emergency alerts or coordination with local authorities. Create a list of these channels and distribute it to all participants. It's also important to assign roles and responsibilities to each person. For example, designate a primary communicator, someone responsible for checking in on family members and another for monitoring emergency channels.

Developing a family communication plan involves teaching everyone how to use the radios effectively. Conduct training sessions to familiarize each family member with the basics of radio operation, including turning the radio on and off, selecting channels, adjusting the volume and using emergency features. Practice using common phrases and codes to streamline communication and ensure that messages are clear and concise.

For a community plan, coordination and cooperation are key. Organize meetings with community members to discuss the communication plan and distribute radios. During these meetings, explain the importance of having a reliable communication network and how it can help during emergencies. Establish a communication tree, where each member is responsible for checking in with a few others, ensuring that everyone stays informed and connected.

Regular drills are essential to maintaining an effective communication plan. Schedule periodic practice sessions where everyone uses their radios to simulate different emergency scenarios. These drills help participants become more comfortable with the equipment and protocols, identify any issues that need addressing and reinforce the importance of the communication plan. After each drill, gather feedback and make necessary adjustments to improve the plan.

Creating emergency contact cards is another important step. These cards should include the primary and secondary communication channels, important contact numbers and basic instructions for using the radios. Distribute these cards to all family members and community participants, then ensure they are kept in accessible locations, such as wallets, emergency kits or near the radios.

Establishing a meeting point is crucial in case of an emergency where evacuation is necessary. Decide on a primary and a secondary location where family members or community participants can gather if communication via radio is not possible. Make sure everyone knows these locations and can reach them safely.

In addition to programming local emergency frequencies, consider programming weather channels into your radios. This allows you to receive real-time updates on weather conditions, which can be crucial during natural disasters like hurricanes or severe storms. Staying informed about weather changes helps in making timely decisions and taking appropriate actions.

Battery management is an often-overlooked aspect of maintaining an emergency communication plan.

Ensure that all radios are kept charged and have spare batteries available. Encourage participants to regularly check their radios to confirm they are working properly. For longer-term preparedness, consider solar chargers or hand-crank chargers to keep radios operational during extended power outages.

Collaboration with local emergency services can enhance the effectiveness of your communication plan. Reach out to local police, fire departments, and emergency medical services to inform them about your community's communication plan and explore ways to integrate your efforts with theirs. Some areas may allow community groups to coordinate directly with emergency services via radio, providing an additional layer of support during crises.

Finally, education and awareness are key components of a successful emergency communication plan. Regularly update all participants on any changes to the plan, new frequencies or additional protocols. Encourage continuous learning and adaptation to new technologies or best practices in emergency communication. Keeping everyone informed and prepared helps build a resilient and responsive community.

In summary, setting up an emergency communication plan using Baofeng radios involves selecting the right equipment, programming the radios with appropriate frequencies, establishing clear communication protocols and conducting regular training and drills. By involving family members and community participants in the process, ensuring proper battery management and collaborating with local emergency services, you can create a robust and reliable communication network that enhances safety and coordination during emergencies. Regular updates and continuous education ensure that the plan remains effective and responsive to evolving needs and situations.

Communicating During Natural Disasters

During natural disasters like hurricanes, earthquakes and floods, communication is crucial for safety and coordination. Baofeng radios can be valuable tools in these situations, providing reliable communication when other methods fail. Here are detailed instructions on using Baofeng radios during natural disasters, along with tips for maintaining communication and safety.

1. Before the Disaster

   - Ensure that all family members or community participants have access to a Baofeng radio and are familiar with its operation.

   - Program the radios with relevant frequencies, including local emergency channels, weather channels and designated family or community channels.

- Conduct drills and practice using the radios to simulate different disaster scenarios, ensuring that everyone knows how to operate them effectively.

- Keep spare batteries, chargers, and accessories like earpieces and antennas in your emergency kit.

2. During the Disaster

- If you receive advance warning of an impending disaster, check that your radios are fully charged and within reach.

- Monitor weather updates on your Baofeng radio to stay informed about the situation and any evacuation orders or alerts.

- If evacuation is necessary, take your Baofeng radio with you and ensure that everyone in your group has one.

- If you are staying at home or in a shelter, keep your radio turned on and tuned to local emergency channels for updates and instructions.

3. Maintaining Communication

- Designate a primary communication channel for your family or community and ensure that everyone knows which channel to use.

- Establish communication protocols, such as check-in times or specific phrases for different situations, to streamline communication and avoid confusion.

- Use simple and clear language when communicating over the radio, keeping messages brief and to the point.

- Regularly check in with family members or community participants to ensure everyone is safe and accounted for.

- If you encounter difficulties reaching someone on the radio, try different channels or locations to improve signal reception.

4. Safety Tips

- Stay indoors and away from windows during hurricanes or severe storms to avoid injury from flying debris.

- If you are evacuating, follow designated evacuation routes and listen to instructions from local authorities.

- In earthquake-prone areas, drop, cover, and hold on during shaking, then use your radio to call for help if needed.

- Be aware of potential hazards like downed power lines, flooding, or unstable structures, and use caution when navigating your surroundings.

- If you are trapped or injured, use your radio to call for assistance and provide your location and condition to rescuers.

5. After the Disaster

- Use your Baofeng radio to communicate with family members, neighbors or emergency services to report damage or request assistance.

- Be patient and persistent when trying to reach someone on the radio, as network congestion or damage to infrastructure may cause delays.

- Listen for updates and instructions from local authorities on your radio and follow their guidance for recovery efforts.

- If you are safe and able to do so, offer assistance to others in your community who may need help or support.

6. Additional Tips

- Use accessories like earpieces or external antennas to improve audio quality and signal reception, especially in noisy or remote environments.

- Keep your radio protected from water, dust, and extreme temperatures to ensure it remains functional during emergencies.

- Practice good radio etiquette, including waiting for a clear channel before transmitting and avoiding unnecessary chatter that could disrupt emergency communications.

- Familiarize yourself with local emergency procedures and resources, such as evacuation routes, emergency shelters and contact numbers for emergency services.

By following these instructions and tips, you can effectively use Baofeng radios during natural disasters to maintain communication, coordinate response efforts, and ensure the safety of yourself and others. Remember to stay calm, stay informed and stay connected during emergencies, and use your radio responsibly to maximize its effectiveness as a lifesaving tool.

Staying Informed: Monitoring Emergency Broadcasts and Weather Channels

Using Baofeng radios to monitor emergency broadcasts and weather channels is a straightforward process that can help keep you informed and prepared during emergencies. Baofeng radios come equipped with a built-in FM radio receiver, allowing you to tune in to local stations for emergency updates and weather forecasts. Additionally, you can program specific frequencies into your radio to access dedicated emergency channels and weather stations.

To monitor emergency broadcasts and weather channels on your Baofeng radio, start by familiarizing yourself with the FM radio function. Locate the FM radio mode on your radio and switch to it using the mode selection button. Once in FM mode, use the tuning knob or keypad to select the desired frequency. Scan through the FM band to find local stations that broadcast emergency alerts and weather updates.

Many Baofeng radios also feature a function called "VFO mode," which allows you to manually input specific frequencies for monitoring. To use VFO mode, enter the desired frequency using the keypad or tuning knob. Consult your local emergency management agency or weather service for the frequencies of dedicated emergency channels and weather stations in your area. These frequencies may vary depending on your location and the services available in your region.

In addition to FM radio and VFO mode, Baofeng radios can be programmed with specific frequencies for emergency channels and weather stations. Using software like Chirp or manually programming the frequencies into your radio, you can ensure quick access to these channels during emergencies. Consult local authorities or emergency management agencies for the recommended frequencies to program into your radio.

Once you have programmed the frequencies into your Baofeng radio, accessing emergency broadcasts and weather channels is as simple as selecting the appropriate channel from your radio's memory. Store the frequencies of important channels in your radio's memory for easy access during emergencies. Label the channels with descriptive names to quickly identify their purpose.

When monitoring emergency broadcasts and weather channels on your Baofeng radio, pay attention to any alerts or updates issued by local authorities or weather services. Listen for information on severe weather warnings, evacuation orders, road closures and other emergency situations that may affect your safety. Follow the instructions provided by authorities and take appropriate actions to protect yourself and your family.

In summary, Baofeng radios can be used to monitor emergency broadcasts and weather channels by tuning in to FM radio stations, using VFO mode to manually input frequencies or programming specific frequencies into the radio's memory. Stay informed by listening for updates and alerts from local authorities and weather services during emergencies. By staying vigilant and prepared, you can effectively use your Baofeng radio to stay informed and stay safe during emergencies.

CHAPTER 6

Legal and Ethical Considerations

Understanding FCC Regulations and Licensing Requirements

Understanding the FCC regulations and licensing requirements for using Baofeng radios is crucial to ensure you operate these devices legally and responsibly. The Federal Communications Commission (FCC) regulates radio communications in the United States to prevent interference and maintain orderly use of the radio spectrum. Baofeng radios, which are popular for their affordability and versatility, can be used under several radio services regulated by the FCC, including the Family Radio Service (FRS), General Mobile Radio Service (GMRS), and Amateur Radio Service (HAM).

Here's a detailed guide to help you navigate these regulations and obtain the necessary licenses.

The FCC governs the use of radio frequencies through a set of rules designed to prevent interference and ensure efficient use of the spectrum. These rules are outlined in various parts of the FCC's regulations, specifically Parts 95 and 97 for personal and amateur radio services, respectively. Baofeng radios can operate on different bands, understanding which service you are using will determine whether you need a license and what kind of restrictions apply.

Family Radio Service (FRS)
FRS is intended for short-distance, personal and family communications. FRS radios typically operate on 22 specific channels in the 462 and 467 MHz bands. These radios have a maximum power output of 2 watts and do not require a license to operate. FRS is designed for ease of use and is suitable for activities like hiking, camping or

coordinating with family members in a neighborhood. Since FRS is a license-free service, anyone can use it, including children, as long as they adhere to the power limits and use the designated channels.

General Mobile Radio Service (GMRS)

GMRS is similar to FRS but allows for higher power outputs, which means greater range. GMRS radios can operate with up to 50 watts of power and can use repeaters to extend their range even further. GMRS also uses the 462 and 467 MHz bands but includes additional frequencies not available to FRS users. Unlike FRS, GMRS requires a license from the FCC. The GMRS license is valid for ten years and covers the licensee and their immediate family members. To obtain a GMRS license, you need to complete FCC Form 605 and pay the required fee. No test is required for this license, making it accessible to most people.

Amateur Radio Service (HAM)

The Amateur Radio Service, commonly known as HAM radio, offers the most flexibility and range among personal radio services. HAM radio operators or "hams," can use a wide range of frequencies across multiple bands and can communicate over very long distances, even globally. However, HAM radio requires a license, and there are three levels of licensing: Technician, General and Amateur Extra. Each level grants access to more frequencies and higher power levels. To obtain a HAM radio license, you must pass an exam that tests your knowledge of radio theory, regulations and operating practices. The exams are administered by volunteer examiners (VEs) affiliated with the FCC.

Understanding and Obtaining Licenses

1. FRS: As mentioned, FRS does not require a license. Simply purchase an FRS-capable Baofeng radio, ensure it operates within the legal parameters

(2 watts or less) and you are ready to communicate on the designated channels.

2. GMRS: To operate on GMRS frequencies, you need to obtain a GMRS license from the FCC. The process involves:

- Visiting the FCC's Universal Licensing System (ULS) website.

- Creating an FCC Registration Number (FRN) if you don't already have one.

- Completing FCC Form 605, which is the application for a GMRS license.

- Paying the licensing fee, which is currently around $70 for a ten-year license.

- Once the application is submitted and the fee is paid, the FCC will process your application and you will receive your license electronically.

3. HAM Radio: Getting a HAM radio license requires passing an exam. Here's how you can get started:

- Study for the exam using resources available online or from local HAM radio clubs. The Technician class license, which is the entry-level, requires knowledge of basic radio theory, operating practices and FCC regulations.

- Schedule your exam with a volunteer examiner coordinator (VEC). The American Radio Relay League (ARRL) and other organizations provide information on how to find a testing session near you.

- Take and pass the Technician exam. Upon passing, you will be granted a call sign and can begin operating on the frequencies permitted for Technician class licensees.

- If desired, you can continue studying and pass additional exams to obtain General and Amateur Extra class licenses, which allow access to more frequencies and higher power levels.

Ethical Considerations and Responsible Use

Adhering to FCC regulations is not just about legality; it also involves ethical considerations to ensure responsible use of the radio spectrum. Here are some key ethical practices:

- **Avoid Interference:** Use only the frequencies and power levels you are authorized to use. Interfering with other communications, whether intentional or accidental, can disrupt critical services and is illegal.

- **Privacy and Respect:** Respect the privacy of other users. Do not listen in on private conversations or use the radio for malicious purposes. Avoid transmitting inappropriate or offensive content.

- **Emergency Communications:** Radio communication is vital during emergencies. Use your radio responsibly to facilitate communication and help others. Familiarize yourself with emergency frequencies and protocols.

- **Equipment Maintenance:** Regularly check and maintain your radio equipment to ensure it operates correctly. Poorly maintained equipment can cause interference and reduce the efficiency of the spectrum.

- **Continuous Learning:** Stay informed about changes in regulations and best practices. Engage with the radio community to share knowledge and experiences.

International Regulations:
While this guide focuses on FCC regulations in the United States, similar regulatory bodies exist in other countries. Each country has its own set of rules and licensing requirements. For example:
- In Canada, Industry Canada (IC) regulates radio communications.
- In the United Kingdom, Ofcom oversees radio communication.
- In Australia, the Australian Communications and Media Authority (ACMA) is the regulatory body.

Research and understand the specific requirements in your country to ensure you comply with local laws and regulations. Many countries also participate in international agreements, such as those coordinated by the International

Telecommunication Union (ITU), to manage the global use of radio frequencies.

Understanding FCC regulations and licensing requirements is essential for using Baofeng radios legally and ethically. By familiarizing yourself with the rules governing FRS, GMRS and HAM radio services, then obtaining the necessary licenses, you can enjoy the benefits of radio communication while complying with legal standards. Whether you're using your Baofeng radio for personal communication, emergency preparedness or as a hobby, responsible and informed use helps maintain the integrity and efficiency of the radio spectrum for everyone. Engage with the broader radio community, stay updated on regulatory changes and continue to educate yourself to ensure your radio use remains compliant and beneficial.

Ethical Use of Two-Way Radios

When using two-way radios, understanding and adhering to ethical considerations is as important as following legal regulations. These practices ensure respectful, efficient and interference-free communication. Here are some key ethical considerations for two-way radio users.

Respecting privacy is fundamental. Two-way radios often operate on shared frequencies, which means multiple users can access the same channels. Conversations that take place over these radios can be easily overheard by others. Therefore, it's important to avoid transmitting sensitive or private information that could compromise personal or professional privacy. Always assume that your communication might be heard by unintended listeners and maintain a level of discretion in what you share.

Avoiding interference is another critical ethical practice. Two-way radios can cause interference if not used correctly, potentially disrupting other communications. This is particularly important in environments like emergency services, aviation and public events, where clear and uninterrupted communication is vital. To minimize interference, use only the power level necessary for your communication and avoid using frequencies for which you are not authorized. When communicating, keep transmissions concise and clear to free up the channel for others.

Proper etiquette also plays a significant role in ethical radio use. Use established communication protocols, such as identifying yourself at the beginning of each transmission and acknowledging when you have received a message. This helps prevent confusion and ensures that messages are clearly understood. Avoid using slang or inappropriate language and be mindful of your tone, especially in professional or emergency contexts.

Emergency communication deserves special attention. During emergencies, two-way radios can be a lifeline, providing critical information and coordination. When an emergency is declared, non-essential communications should cease immediately to keep the channel open for emergency traffic. If you come across an emergency transmission, stop all other communications and listen to provide assistance if needed. Misuse of emergency channels is not only unethical but can also be dangerous and is often illegal.

Additionally, responsible equipment use and maintenance are essential. Ensure your radio equipment is functioning correctly to prevent accidental interference or transmission failures. Regularly check your device for any technical issues, such as battery life, signal clarity and proper tuning. Using malfunctioning equipment can lead to unintended disruptions and communication breakdowns.

Another important ethical consideration is environmental impact. Many two-way radios use batteries, which can be harmful to the environment if not disposed of properly. Use rechargeable batteries when possible to reduce waste and always follow local regulations for battery disposal. Additionally, consider the impact of your communication practices on wildlife, especially when operating in natural or protected areas. Excessive noise or interference can disturb animals and disrupt their habitats.

Ethical use also involves education and awareness. Stay informed about the rules and best practices for radio communication. Participate in training sessions or join radio clubs where you can learn from experienced operators. Sharing knowledge and promoting ethical practices within the radio community helps ensure that all users can communicate effectively and responsibly.

Community respect is another aspect of ethical radio use. Recognize that two-way radio frequencies are a shared resource. Be patient and courteous when waiting for a clear channel and avoid monopolizing frequencies with unnecessary chatter. If you hear other users experiencing difficulties, offer assistance if you can do so without causing additional disruption. Building a supportive and respectful radio community enhances the overall experience for everyone involved.

Promoting inclusivity and accessibility in radio communication is important. Encourage and support new users, helping them understand both the technical and ethical aspects of using two-way radios. Create an environment where all users, regardless of their experience level, feel welcome and able to contribute. By fostering a culture of respect and collaboration, the radio community can thrive and provide a valuable service to its members and the broader public.

Ethical use of two-way radios involves respecting privacy, avoiding interference, following proper etiquette, prioritizing emergency communication, maintaining equipment responsibly, considering environmental impact, staying educated, respecting the community and promoting inclusivity. By adhering to these principles, radio users can ensure their communications are effective, respectful and beneficial to all.

Privacy Concerns and Best Practices

Two-way radios are invaluable tools for communication in various settings, but they come with certain privacy concerns. Understanding these concerns and implementing best practices for maintaining privacy and security is crucial for safe and effective use.

One of the primary privacy concerns with two-way radios is that they operate on open frequencies, meaning that anyone with a similar device can potentially listen in on conversations. This lack of encryption makes it easy for unauthorized listeners to intercept communications, leading to potential breaches of sensitive information. To mitigate this risk, users should avoid discussing confidential or sensitive topics over the radio. Instead, they should reserve such conversations for more secure communication methods, such as encrypted messaging apps or face-to-face meetings.

Another privacy concern is the accidental sharing of personal information. In the heat of communication, especially during emergencies or busy events, users might inadvertently transmit personal details like names, addresses or phone numbers. To prevent this, it's important to develop a habit of using code words or pre-arranged signals to convey sensitive information. For example, instead of saying a full address, you might use a predefined code that only your group understands.

Channel privacy is another significant issue. Many users may share the same frequencies, leading to overlapping communications and potential eavesdropping. Using Continuous Tone-Coded Squelch System (CTCSS) or Digital Coded Squelch (DCS) can help filter out unwanted communications by using specific sub-audible tones. While these tones do not provide true encryption, they can reduce the likelihood of interference from other users on the same frequency.

To further enhance privacy, regularly changing frequencies or channels can be an effective strategy. This practice, known as frequency hopping, makes it harder for unauthorized listeners to follow conversations. However, it requires coordination among all users to ensure everyone is on the same channel at the same time. Pre-planning and clear protocols for frequency changes are essential to avoid confusion.

Using earpieces and headsets is another practical measure to maintain privacy. These accessories prevent the audio from the radio from being heard by nearby individuals, which is particularly useful in crowded or public areas. They also allow for hands-free operation, making it easier to communicate discreetly.

For those using Baofeng or similar radios, programming the radios to use the lowest effective power setting can help limit the range of your transmissions, reducing the risk of unauthorized interception. Higher power settings increase the range but also make your communications more accessible to distant eavesdroppers.

It's also important to regularly update the firmware of your radio devices, if applicable. Manufacturers sometimes release updates that enhance security features or fix vulnerabilities. Staying current with these updates can provide better protection against privacy breaches.

When it comes to group communications, establishing clear communication protocols is crucial. This includes deciding on specific times or conditions for radio use, agreeing on the use of code words and setting guidelines for handling sensitive information. Training all users on these protocols ensures that everyone is aware of the best practices and adheres to them consistently.

Another best practice is conducting regular security audits of your radio communication setup. This involves reviewing and assessing the current practices, checking for any vulnerabilities, and updating protocols as necessary. Regular audits help to identify and mitigate potential risks before they become significant problems.

Educating users about the importance of radio etiquette and privacy is fundamental. Providing training sessions and resources can help users understand the potential risks and the steps they can take to protect their communications. Awareness is the first line of defense against privacy breaches.

In summary, maintaining privacy and security while using two-way radios involves a combination of avoiding sensitive topics, using coded language, employing CTCSS/DCS, regularly changing frequencies, using earpieces, setting low power transmissions, updating firmware, establishing communication protocols, conducting security audits and educating users. By implementing these best practices, users can significantly enhance the privacy and security of their radio communications.

Avoiding Interference with Public Services

Two-way radios are powerful tools for communication, but they must be used responsibly to avoid interfering with public services such as police, fire and medical channels. Interference with these services can have serious legal and practical consequences, making it essential for radio users to understand and comply with regulations.

Public services like police, fire and emergency medical services operate on designated radio frequencies to ensure clear, reliable communication during critical situations. These frequencies are often reserved and protected by law, meaning unauthorized use can disrupt vital operations, leading to potentially dangerous outcomes. To avoid interference, users must first be aware of the specific frequencies allocated for public service use in their region. This information is typically available through national regulatory bodies like the Federal Communications Commission (FCC) in the United States.

Using only authorized frequencies is the first step in preventing interference. Two-way radios, including Baofeng models, can often be programmed to access a wide range of frequencies. However, users should never program their radios to operate on frequencies reserved for public services unless they have explicit permission and the necessary licenses. Transmitting on these frequencies without authorization is illegal and can result in severe penalties, including fines and imprisonment.

Understanding and adhering to the rules set by regulatory bodies like the FCC is crucial. The FCC allocates specific frequency bands for different types of users, including commercial, personal and public safety. It is the responsibility of radio users to ensure their devices are configured to operate within the legal frequency ranges assigned for their intended use. For example, Family Radio Service (FRS) and General Mobile Radio Service (GMRS) channels are available for personal use in the U.S., while specific bands are reserved for public safety.

Regularly updating the firmware and software of your radio devices can also help prevent interference. Manufacturers may release updates that improve frequency control and reduce the risk of unintentional transmissions on restricted channels. Staying current with these updates ensures that your device operates within the correct parameters.

Proper training and education on radio use are essential for compliance. Users should understand how to set and lock their radios to approved channels. Many radios have a channel lock feature that prevents accidental switching to unauthorized frequencies. Learning how to use these features effectively can help minimize the risk of interference.

Listening before transmitting is a basic but important practice. Always ensure the channel is clear before you start transmitting. This practice helps avoid interrupting ongoing communications, which can be particularly critical on shared or congested frequencies. Using the squelch control on your radio can help filter out background noise and identify when a channel is in use.

In areas where public service channels are actively used, keeping transmissions short and to the point reduces the chance of interference. Extended conversations on any frequency can cause congestion and increase the risk of accidental overlap with public service channels. Practice concise communication and encourage others in your group to do the same.

Monitoring the output power of your transmissions can also prevent interference. Most two-way radios allow users to adjust the power output. Lower power settings are usually sufficient for short-range communication and help minimize the reach of your transmissions, reducing the likelihood of interfering with distant public service operations. Reserve higher power settings for when they are absolutely necessary and appropriate.

Educating your radio group or community about the importance of avoiding interference with public services is crucial. Sharing knowledge about legal frequencies, proper usage protocols and the potential consequences of interference can promote responsible radio use. Encourage open discussions and regular training sessions to keep everyone informed and compliant.

In emergency situations, where communication needs might be heightened, maintaining discipline is even more important. Refrain from using radios for non-essential communication and ensure all users are aware of the critical nature of clear channels during emergencies. This practice helps ensure that public service communications remain uninterrupted and effective.

If you suspect or discover that you have accidentally interfered with a public service frequency, it's important to cease transmissions immediately and report the incident to the appropriate authorities. Taking responsibility and cooperating with regulatory bodies can mitigate the consequences and help resolve any issues swiftly.

Avoiding interference with public services when using two-way radios involves using only authorized frequencies, staying updated with regulations, proper training and education, listening before transmitting, keeping transmissions concise, monitoring power output and promoting responsible use within your community. Understanding and adhering to these practices not only ensures compliance with the law but also supports the vital work of emergency and public safety services, helping them operate efficiently and effectively.

CHAPTER 7

Troubleshooting and Maintenance

Common Issues and Quick Fixes

Baofeng radios are reliable tools, but like any technology, they can experience issues. Understanding common problems and knowing how to troubleshoot them can save time and ensure effective communication. Here are some frequent issues users might encounter with Baofeng radios, along with troubleshooting tips and quick fixes.

A common issue is poor audio quality or static during transmissions. This can often be caused by interference or obstacles between the radios. To fix this, try changing your location to a higher elevation or a more open area. Check the antenna to ensure it is securely attached and in good condition. If the problem persists, consider using a different frequency or channel to see if the issue is specific to a particular frequency.

Another frequent problem is the radio not turning on. This is usually related to battery issues. First, check that the battery is properly installed and fully charged. If the battery is old, it may need to be replaced. Ensure that the battery contacts are clean and free of corrosion. If you are using a charger, confirm that it is functioning correctly and providing power. Sometimes, a reset of the radio by removing and reinserting the battery can solve the issue.

Users often encounter difficulties with transmitting or receiving signals. If you can't transmit, check that the radio is set to the correct frequency and that the frequency is not restricted or reserved for other uses. Ensure that the push-to-talk (PTT) button is functioning properly. If receiving is the issue, make sure the volume is turned up and the squelch setting is properly adjusted. Also, verify that the radio is not in "mute" mode or set to a privacy code that other radios in your group are not using.

Programming issues are another common challenge, especially for new users. If you're having trouble programming frequencies manually, refer to the user manual for step-by-step instructions. Using software like Chirp can simplify the programming process. Ensure that you have the correct programming cable and that it is securely connected. Double-check that you are entering the frequencies correctly and that they are within the legal bands for your use.

Battery life concerns are also prevalent. If your battery is draining quickly, check if the radio is transmitting more often than necessary, as this uses more power. Reduce the power output setting if possible and turn off any features you are not using, such as the backlight or scan functions. If you frequently use the radio, consider having spare batteries or a higher capacity battery pack available.

Sometimes, users may find that their radios are not communicating with each other. This can be due to the radios not being on the same frequency or privacy code. Ensure that all radios in your group are programmed with the same settings. Verify that the channel, frequency and any CTCSS or DCS codes match. If using dual-band radios, make sure all users are on the same band (VHF or UHF).

Antenna problems can also affect performance. If you notice a significant drop in range or signal quality, check the antenna for damage or wear. Ensure it is securely connected to the radio. Using an upgraded antenna can sometimes improve performance, especially in challenging environments.

Users might also encounter issues with accessories such as earpieces or microphones. If an accessory is not working, first check that it is properly connected to the radio. Test the accessory on another radio if possible to determine if the issue is with the accessory or the radio. Ensure that any connections are clean and free of debris.

Firmware and software issues can sometimes cause problems. Regularly check for updates from the manufacturer and apply them as necessary. Updates can fix bugs and improve the performance of your radio. Ensure you follow the update instructions carefully to avoid bricking the device.

Common issues with Baofeng radios include poor audio quality, power problems, transmission and reception difficulties, programming challenges, battery life concerns, communication mismatches, antenna problems, accessory malfunctions and firmware issues. Troubleshooting these problems involves checking battery and antenna connections, adjusting settings, verifying programming, updating software and ensuring proper use of accessories.

Understanding these common issues and their fixes can help you maintain your Baofeng radio in good working order, ensuring reliable communication when you need it most.

Maintaining Battery Health and Longevity

Maintaining and extending the battery life of Baofeng radios is essential for reliable communication, especially in critical situations. Proper care and usage can significantly prolong battery health and efficiency. Here are some practical tips and best practices for charging, storage and overall battery maintenance.

One of the primary ways to extend battery life is to charge the battery correctly. Always use the charger that came with your Baofeng radio or a compatible, high-quality alternative. Charging with inappropriate or substandard chargers can damage the battery and reduce its lifespan. Follow the manufacturer's instructions for charging times.

Typically, the first charge should be longer to condition the battery, usually about 12 hours, while subsequent charges can follow regular guidelines, often around 3-5 hours.

Avoid overcharging the battery. Although modern batteries and chargers often have protection circuits to prevent overcharging, it's still a good practice to unplug the charger once the battery is fully charged. Leaving the battery connected to the charger for extended periods, even with protection circuits, can lead to heat build-up, which degrades battery health over time.

Maintaining an optimal charge level is also crucial. For lithium-ion batteries, which are commonly used in Baofeng radios, keeping the charge between 20% and 80% can help extend battery life. Completely draining the battery or keeping it fully charged for long periods can stress the battery cells. Regularly charging the battery before it drops below 20% can prevent deep discharges that are harmful to lithium-ion batteries.

Storing the battery properly when it is not in use is another key factor. If you plan to store the battery for an extended period, make sure it is charged to about 50%. Storing a battery fully charged or fully discharged can lead to capacity loss. Store the battery in a cool, dry place, away from direct sunlight and extreme temperatures. High temperatures can accelerate the aging process of the battery, while very low temperatures can reduce its performance temporarily.

Regular use and proper cycling of the battery are beneficial. Batteries that are left unused for long periods can lose their ability to hold a charge effectively. If you have spare batteries, rotate their use to ensure all of them remain in good condition. This practice helps maintain the battery's chemical balance and keeps it functioning optimally.

Temperature management during charging and use is important. Avoid charging the battery in very hot or very cold environments. Charging at room temperature is ideal, as extreme temperatures can affect the charging efficiency and battery health. Similarly, using the radio in moderate temperatures helps maintain battery performance and longevity.

Using power-saving features on your Baofeng radio can help extend battery life during operation. Most radios come with features like battery saver mode, which reduces power consumption when the radio is idle. Adjusting the power output setting to the lowest effective level for your communication needs can also conserve battery life. High power settings drain the battery faster, so use high power only when necessary for long-range communication.

Monitor the battery's health regularly. Pay attention to signs of wear, such as the battery not holding a charge as well as it used to or the radio shutting off unexpectedly. If you notice these signs, it may be time to replace the battery. Using a battery analyzer or tester can help you assess the health of your battery more accurately.

Avoid physical damage to the battery. Dropping the radio or battery can cause internal damage that may not be immediately apparent but can lead to reduced performance or even safety hazards. Handle the battery and radio with care to avoid impacts that could affect the battery's integrity.

Maintaining and extending the battery life of Baofeng radios involves proper charging practices, avoiding overcharging, keeping the battery at an optimal charge level, proper storage, regular use, temperature management, utilizing power-saving features, monitoring battery health and handling the battery carefully. By following these best practices, you can ensure your Baofeng radio's battery remains reliable and efficient, providing you with dependable communication whenever you need it.

Cleaning and Caring for Your Baofeng Radio

Proper cleaning and maintenance of Baofeng radios are crucial for ensuring their longevity and optimal performance. Regular care helps prevent damage and keeps the radios functioning efficiently. Here are detailed instructions for cleaning and maintaining your Baofeng radio.

Start by turning off the radio and removing the battery. This prevents any electrical issues or accidental transmissions while cleaning. Make sure the radio is not connected to a charger or any external accessories. Removing the battery also allows you to clean the battery contacts thoroughly, which is essential for maintaining a good connection and ensuring reliable power.

Use a soft, dry cloth to wipe down the exterior of the radio. This removes any dust or light dirt that may have accumulated on the surface. For more stubborn dirt or grime, slightly dampen the cloth with water. Avoid using excessive water, as moisture can damage the electronic components inside the radio. Gently wipe all surfaces, including the buttons, display screen and antenna.

For areas with accumulated dirt or grime, such as the crevices around buttons or the microphone, use a soft brush or a cotton swab. A small, soft-bristled brush, like a toothbrush, can effectively clean these tight spaces without scratching the surface. Dip the brush or cotton swab in a mixture of mild soap and water if needed, but ensure it is only slightly damp. Carefully clean around the buttons and other crevices, removing any buildup that could interfere with the radio's functionality.

Cleaning the antenna is also important. Unscrew the antenna from the radio and wipe it down with a soft cloth. If the antenna has threads, use a dry brush or cloth to clean them and remove any dust or debris. Ensure the connection points are clean before reattaching the antenna to the radio. A clean antenna ensures better signal transmission and reception.

Inspect the battery contacts for any signs of corrosion or dirt. Clean the contacts with a dry cloth or a cotton swab dipped in isopropyl alcohol. This helps remove any residue that might interfere with the electrical connection. Ensure the contacts are completely dry before reinserting the battery into the radio. Regular cleaning of the battery contacts helps maintain efficient power transfer and prolongs battery life.

When cleaning the display screen, use a microfiber cloth to avoid scratching the surface. Avoid using harsh chemicals or abrasive materials, as they can damage the screen. If necessary, lightly dampen the microfiber cloth with water or a screen-cleaning solution specifically designed for electronic displays. Gently wipe the screen to remove fingerprints, smudges, and dust.

Periodic checks and maintenance of the radio's accessories, such as earpieces, microphones and chargers, are also important. Clean these accessories using the same methods; soft cloths, brushes and mild cleaning solutions. Ensure that all connectors and plugs are free of dirt and corrosion to maintain good electrical contact. Proper care of accessories contributes to the overall performance and longevity of your Baofeng radio.

Preventative maintenance is key to keeping your Baofeng radio in good working condition. Store the radio in a cool, dry place when not in use. Avoid exposing it to extreme temperatures, moisture or direct sunlight, as these conditions can damage the internal components and reduce the radio's lifespan. Using a protective case or cover can also help prevent physical damage from drops or impacts.

Regularly check the radio for any signs of wear or damage. Look for cracks, loose parts or other physical damage that might affect performance. Address any issues promptly to prevent further damage. If you notice any problems that you cannot fix yourself, consider taking the radio to a professional technician for repair.

Software updates and firmware maintenance are also part of keeping your Baofeng radio in top condition. Check the manufacturer's website or user manuals for any available updates. Updating the software can fix bugs, improve performance and add new features. Follow the instructions carefully to ensure a successful update without damaging the radio.

Proper cleaning and maintenance of Baofeng radios involve turning off the radio and removing the battery, using soft cloths and brushes to clean the exterior and crevices, cleaning the antenna and battery contacts, using a microfiber cloth for the display screen and performing regular checks and preventative maintenance. By following these steps, you can ensure your Baofeng radio remains in excellent condition, providing reliable communication and optimal performance for a long time.

Upgrading Firmware and Software

Upgrading the firmware and software of your Baofeng radio is essential for ensuring the latest features, improved performance and enhanced security. The process may seem daunting, but with clear instructions, you can perform these upgrades confidently. Here's a comprehensive guide to help you through the process.

Begin by identifying the model of your Baofeng radio. Different models may have specific firmware or software versions, so it's crucial to ensure you are using the correct files. Check the user manual or the label on the radio for the model number. Common Baofeng models include the UV-5R, BF-F8HP and UV-82.

Next, visit the Baofeng website or the website of your radio's distributor to find the appropriate firmware and software updates. Look for a support or downloads section where you can find the latest updates for your specific model. Download the firmware file and any necessary software to your computer. Ensure you download from a reputable source to avoid malware or corrupted files.

Before you start the upgrade process, back up any important settings or configurations from your radio. This step is crucial in case something goes wrong during the upgrade. If you have customized channels or settings, use software like CHIRP to save these settings to your computer. Open CHIRP, connect your radio and download the current configuration. Save this file in a safe location.

To connect your radio to the computer, you'll need a USB programming cable compatible with your Baofeng model. These cables are usually available from the same place where you bought your radio or from other electronics retailers. Connect the cable to your radio and plug the other end into a USB port on your computer. Ensure the radio is turned off before connecting.

Install any necessary drivers for the programming cable. These drivers allow your computer to communicate with the radio through the USB port. Drivers are typically available from the same source as the firmware and software updates. Follow the installation instructions provided with the driver files.

Once the drivers are installed, open the firmware update software on your computer. This software is usually provided by Baofeng or your radio's distributor. Follow the instructions to load the firmware file you downloaded earlier. Make sure your radio is still turned off and connected to the computer.

Turn on your radio while holding down specific buttons to enter firmware update mode. The buttons you need to press may vary by model, so refer to your user manual or the instructions provided with the firmware update software. For many Baofeng models, holding down the "PTT" (Push-To-Talk) and "Monitor" buttons while turning on the radio will enter update mode.

With the radio in update mode, start the firmware update process in the software. This step may take several minutes. It is crucial not to disconnect the radio or interrupt the process during the update. Interrupting the firmware update can cause the radio to become inoperable.

After the firmware update is complete, turn off the radio and disconnect it from the computer. Turn the radio back on normally to ensure it boots up correctly with the new firmware. Check the firmware version on the radio to confirm the update was successful. This information is typically found in the settings menu or can be displayed on the startup screen.

If you backed up your radio's settings before the update, you can now restore these settings using CHIRP or the software you used for the backup. Connect your radio to the computer, open the backup file and upload the settings back to the radio. This step restores your custom channels and configurations.

It is also a good idea to perform a factory reset after updating the firmware. This step ensures all new settings are properly initialized and any potential conflicts with old settings are resolved. Refer to your user manual for instructions on performing a factory reset specific to your model.

Regularly check for future firmware and software updates to keep your radio functioning at its best. Set a reminder to check the manufacturer's website or join user forums where updates are often discussed and announced. Staying up to date with the latest releases can provide new features, fix bugs and enhance overall performance.

Upgrading the firmware and software of your Baofeng radio involves identifying your model, downloading the correct files, backing up existing settings, connecting the radio to your computer with a programming cable, installing necessary drivers, using the firmware update software and following specific steps to complete the update. Regular maintenance and staying informed about updates will ensure your Baofeng radio operates efficiently and remains reliable for all your communication needs.

CHAPTER 8

Building a Community Network

Connecting with Local Radio Enthusiasts

Building a community network through connecting with local radio enthusiasts is a fulfilling way to enhance your skills and enjoy your Baofeng radio to its fullest potential. Local clubs and groups provide a wealth of knowledge, camaraderie and opportunities for practical experience. Here's how to find and join these groups, and what to expect when you do.

The first step is to identify local radio clubs and groups. Many areas have amateur radio clubs that welcome new members and provide resources for both beginners and experienced users. To find these clubs, you can start by searching online for amateur radio clubs in your city or region. Websites like the American Radio Relay League (ARRL) offer directories of affiliated clubs across the country. You can also check local community bulletin boards, libraries and electronics stores for flyers or notices about radio club meetings.

Once you have identified potential clubs, reach out to them. Most clubs have a website or social media presence with contact information. Send an email or message expressing your interest in joining. Introduce yourself briefly and mention your experience level with Baofeng radios. Clubs are usually very welcoming to newcomers and eager to share their knowledge.

Attending club meetings is a great way to get involved. These meetings are typically held monthly and provide a platform for members to discuss various topics related to amateur radio. Meetings often feature guest speakers, technical presentations and equipment demonstrations. Attending regularly will help you build relationships with other radio enthusiasts and learn more about the hobby.

Participating in club activities is another excellent way to immerse yourself in the community. Many clubs organize events such as field days, where members set up portable radio stations in public areas to practice their skills and demonstrate the hobby to the public. These events provide hands-on experience and are a fun way to spend time with like-minded individuals. Clubs also often participate in contests, emergency communication drills and public service events where radio operators provide communication support for local events like marathons or festivals.

Joining online forums and social media groups dedicated to Baofeng radios and amateur radio can also enhance your experience. Platforms like Reddit, Facebook and specialized forums such as

QRZ.com offer communities where you can ask questions, share experiences and learn from others. These online groups are especially useful for finding answers to specific technical questions or troubleshooting issues you may encounter with your Baofeng radio.

Engaging with local radio enthusiasts can also lead to opportunities for mentorship. Many experienced operators are willing to mentor newcomers, offering guidance on everything from programming your radio to understanding the nuances of different frequencies. A mentor can help you navigate the complexities of amateur radio and provide personalized advice based on their own experiences.

Field trips and collaborative projects are another benefit of joining a local club. Some clubs organize trips to interesting locations for radio operation, such as mountain tops, remote parks or historical sites. These excursions provide a unique setting for practicing your skills and often involve setting up portable antennas and other equipment. Collaborative projects, like building a community repeater or organizing a special event station, foster teamwork and allow you to contribute to a larger goal.

When you join a club or group, be proactive in your participation. Volunteer for roles or tasks, whether it's helping to set up for an event, managing the club's social media page or coordinating a project. Active participation not only enhances your experience but also helps the club thrive and grow. Your contributions, no matter how small, are valuable to the community.

Local clubs also provide resources for obtaining necessary licenses and certifications. In the United States, for example, the ARRL-affiliated clubs often offer classes and testing sessions for the Technician, General and Extra class amateur radio licenses. These classes provide a structured way to learn the material and prepare for the licensing exams.

Successfully obtaining your license not only legalizes your operation but also opens up more frequencies and capabilities for your Baofeng radio.

Another important aspect of connecting with local radio enthusiasts is the opportunity for equipment exchange. Many clubs have members who buy, sell, or trade radio equipment. This can be a cost-effective way to upgrade your setup or acquire additional accessories. Club meetings often include swap meets or auctions where you can find deals on used equipment and parts.

Being part of a community network offers support in times of need. Radio clubs often play a crucial role in emergency communications. During natural disasters or other emergencies, local clubs can provide vital communication links when other systems fail. By being an active member of a club, you can contribute to and benefit from this community support, ensuring you and your community stay connected and informed during crises.

Connecting with local radio enthusiasts through clubs and groups enhances your experience with Baofeng radios by providing education, camaraderie and practical opportunities. By searching for clubs, attending meetings, participating in activities, engaging online, seeking mentorship, volunteering, obtaining licenses and exchanging equipment, you become an integral part of a supportive and knowledgeable community. This network not only enriches your hobby but also strengthens your ability to contribute to and benefit from amateur radio's vital role in communication and public service.

Participating in Ham Radio Clubs and Networks

Joining ham radio clubs and networks offers numerous benefits that enhance your experience with amateur radio, whether you're a novice or an experienced operator. These organizations provide educational resources, foster a sense of community, and offer practical opportunities for learning and service. Here's a detailed look at the advantages of joining these groups and how you can get involved and participate effectively.

One of the primary benefits of joining a ham radio club is access to a wealth of knowledge. Clubs often consist of members with varying levels of expertise, from beginners to seasoned operators. This mix creates an environment where learning is continuous and diverse. Experienced members can offer guidance on technical aspects, such as radio programming, antenna setup and operating procedures. Many clubs also organize training sessions, workshops and guest lectures, which can help you understand complex topics more easily and gain practical skills.

Another significant benefit is the sense of community and camaraderie that comes with club membership. Being part of a group of like-minded individuals who share your interest in ham radio can be incredibly rewarding. Clubs often host regular meetings, social events and field days, providing ample opportunities to build friendships and share experiences. This social aspect can make the hobby more enjoyable and fulfilling, as you can share your successes and troubleshoot issues together.

Clubs and networks also offer numerous practical opportunities for operating and experimentation. Many clubs participate in contests and special events, which can be both fun and challenging. These activities often require coordination and teamwork, allowing you to practice and improve your operating skills. Additionally, clubs may organize projects like building and maintaining repeaters or conducting experiments with different types of antennas and modes. These projects can provide hands-on experience that is invaluable for deepening your understanding of radio technology.

Getting involved in a ham radio club typically begins with finding a club that fits your interests and location. The American Radio Relay League (ARRL) and other national organizations maintain directories of affiliated clubs, which can be searched by location. You can also find clubs through local community centers, online forums, or word of mouth from other radio enthusiasts. Once you've identified a club, reach out via email or phone to express your interest and inquire about attending a meeting or event.

Attending your first club meeting can be an exciting step. Meetings are usually held monthly and offer a chance to meet other members, learn about upcoming events and participate in discussions. When attending a meeting, introduce yourself and share a bit about your experience and interests in ham radio. Don't hesitate to ask questions or seek advice; club members are generally very welcoming and eager to help newcomers.

Participation in club activities is key to getting the most out of your membership. Clubs often host a variety of events, such as field days, where members set up portable stations in outdoor locations to practice emergency communication skills and demonstrate the hobby to the public. Contests are another popular activity, providing a competitive yet friendly environment to test your operating skills against others. Public service events, such as providing communication support for marathons or disaster drills, offer a way to give back to the community while honing your skills.

Joining online networks and forums is another way to participate in the ham radio community. Platforms like QRZ.com, Reddit and Facebook have dedicated groups for ham radio operators, where you can ask questions, share experiences and learn from a global community. These online forums can be especially useful for finding solutions to specific technical issues or staying updated on the latest developments in the hobby.

Mentorship is a valuable aspect of ham radio clubs and networks. Many clubs have programs that pair experienced operators with newcomers to provide one-on-one guidance. A mentor can help you navigate the complexities of obtaining your license, setting up your equipment and understanding the nuances of different operating modes and bands. This personalized support can accelerate your learning and build your confidence as an operator.

Volunteering for club roles or projects is another excellent way to get involved. Clubs often rely on member volunteers to organize events, manage communications, or handle technical tasks like maintaining repeaters. By volunteering, you not only contribute to the club's success but also gain valuable experience and build stronger connections with other members. Even small contributions, such as helping set up for an event or assisting with administrative tasks, can make a big difference.

For those interested in obtaining or upgrading their amateur radio licenses, clubs can provide crucial support. Many clubs offer licensing classes and testing sessions, which can help you prepare for and pass the required exams. These classes typically cover the material in a structured way, making it easier to understand and retain the information. Additionally, club members can offer advice on the licensing process and what to expect during the exams.

Being part of a ham radio club or network enhances your ability to participate in emergency communications. Clubs often work closely with local emergency management agencies and participate in emergency drills and exercises. By being an active member, you can contribute to these efforts and be better prepared to provide communication support during actual emergencies. This role is a significant part of the amateur radio service and underscores the importance of ham radio as a reliable means of communication in times of need.

Joining ham radio clubs and networks provides educational resources, community support, practical operating opportunities and a pathway to mentorship and volunteering. To get involved, start by finding a local club, attend meetings, participate in events, engage with online forums, seek mentorship, volunteer for roles and utilize club resources for licensing and emergency communications. By doing so, you will enrich your experience with amateur radio and become a valued member of a vibrant and supportive community.

Organizing Community Drills and Training Sessions

Organizing and conducting community drills and training sessions using Baofeng radios is a crucial part of ensuring preparedness and effective communication during emergencies. These drills not only help individuals familiarize themselves with radio operations but also build coordination and trust among community members. Here's a detailed guide on how to effectively plan and execute these drills and training sessions.

Begin by understanding the purpose and objectives of the drill or training session. The primary goal is to ensure that all participants know how to use their Baofeng radios efficiently and understand the communication protocols that will be used in an emergency. Define clear objectives, such as familiarizing participants with basic radio operations, testing the communication range and practicing specific emergency scenarios.

Once you have defined your objectives, the next step is to gather and prepare the necessary resources. Ensure that all participants have a working Baofeng radio and understand the basic functions, such as turning it on, setting frequencies and using the push-to-talk button. It's also helpful to have spare radios, batteries and chargers available in case of equipment issues. Prepare printed or digital guides that outline the steps for operating the radios, common frequencies to use and the communication protocols that will be followed during the drill.

Planning the logistics of the drill is essential for smooth execution. Choose a suitable date and time that accommodates the majority of participants. Weekends or evenings might be best for most people. Select a central location that is easily accessible, such as a community center, park or school. If the drill involves multiple locations, ensure that all sites are confirmed and that participants know where to go.

Create a detailed drill plan that outlines the sequence of events. Start with a brief introduction and overview of the objectives, followed by a step-by-step demonstration of the radio operations. This demonstration should cover turning on the radio, adjusting the volume, selecting channels and using any relevant features such as scanning or using CTCSS/DCS codes for privacy. After the demonstration, conduct a hands-on practice session where participants can test their radios and ask questions.

It's important to include specific scenarios in your drill to simulate real-life emergency situations. These scenarios could include a mock evacuation, a search and rescue operation, or coordinating support during a natural disaster. Assign roles to participants, such as incident commander, team leaders and communication officers, to mimic the structure of an actual emergency response team. This role-playing helps participants understand the importance of clear communication and following protocols.

During the drill, encourage participants to practice using proper radio etiquette. This includes speaking clearly and concisely, using call signs to identify themselves and acknowledging messages received.

Emphasize the importance of maintaining a calm and composed demeanor, as this can significantly impact the effectiveness of communication during a real emergency.

To enhance the realism of the drill, introduce elements of surprise and unpredictability. This could involve simulated power outages, unexpected changes in the scenario or additional tasks that require quick thinking and problem-solving. These elements help participants adapt to changing conditions and improve their ability to communicate under pressure.

After the drill, conduct a debriefing session to review the performance and identify areas for improvement. Gather feedback from participants about what went well and what challenges they faced. Discuss any technical issues with the radios, such as signal interference or battery problems and provide solutions for future drills. Use this feedback to refine your plans and make necessary adjustments for subsequent drills.

Regularly scheduled training sessions are also important to maintain and improve the skills learned during drills. These sessions can focus on specific aspects of radio operation, such as programming channels, using repeaters or advanced features like dual watch and dual standby modes. By continually building on the knowledge and skills of participants, you ensure that they remain proficient and confident in using their Baofeng radios.

Promoting the drills and training sessions within the community is essential for maximum participation. Use various communication channels, such as community bulletin boards, social media, email newsletters and word of mouth, to inform residents about upcoming events. Highlight the importance of these drills in enhancing community safety and preparedness.

Collaboration with local emergency services, such as fire departments, police and medical responders, can add significant value to your drills. These professionals can provide insights into real-world emergency communication practices and participate in the drills to create a more comprehensive training experience. Their involvement also helps establish stronger relationships between the community and emergency responders.

Documentation is an important aspect of organizing community drills. Keep records of each drill, including the objectives, participants, scenarios, outcomes and feedback. This documentation helps track progress over time, identify trends and demonstrate the value of these activities to the community and potential funders.

Organizing and conducting community drills and training sessions with Baofeng radios involves careful planning, resource preparation, effective execution and continuous improvement. By setting clear objectives, providing hands-on practice, simulating real-life scenarios and regularly reviewing and refining the process, you can ensure that your community is well-prepared to use Baofeng radios effectively in any emergency situation.

Online Resources and Forums for Continuous Learning

For those interested in expanding their knowledge and staying updated on Baofeng radios and two-way communication, there are numerous online resources, forums and communities that offer valuable information and support. Engaging with these platforms can enhance your understanding, provide practical tips and connect you with other enthusiasts. Here's a comprehensive guide to some of the best online resources available.

One of the most popular and comprehensive resources is the RadioReference website. This site is a treasure trove of information for radio enthusiasts, offering a vast database of frequencies, forums for discussion and a wiki with detailed articles on various radio-related topics. The site's forums are particularly useful for troubleshooting, sharing experiences and asking questions about specific models like the Baofeng UV-5R. The active community includes both beginners and seasoned users who are always willing to help.

The ARRL (American Radio Relay League) website is another invaluable resource. As the national association for amateur radio in the United States, ARRL provides a wealth of information, including articles, guides and educational materials. Their Learning Center offers courses and webinars on a range of topics, from basic radio operation to advanced communication techniques. Membership in ARRL also grants access to their QST magazine, which features in-depth articles and reviews on the latest equipment and technologies.

For those who prefer video tutorials, YouTube hosts a variety of channels dedicated to Baofeng radios and two-way communication. Channels like Ham Radio Crash Course, Tech Minds and NotARubicon Productions provide detailed reviews, how-to guides, and troubleshooting tips. These channels often feature step-by-step instructions that are easy to follow, making them ideal for visual learners. Watching these videos can help you get up to speed quickly and see real-world applications of different features and functions.

Reddit's r/Baofeng and r/amateurradio communities are also excellent places for continuous learning. These subreddits are vibrant forums where users post questions, share tips and discuss the latest developments in the world of two-way radios. The community is welcoming and supportive, making it a great place for beginners to ask questions and learn from more experienced operators. The searchable archives can also be a goldmine of information on common issues and solutions.

The Miklor website is specifically tailored to Baofeng radios, offering detailed manuals, firmware updates and a comprehensive FAQ section. Miklor's guides cover everything from initial setup and programming to advanced features and troubleshooting. The site is user-friendly and regularly updated, ensuring that you have access to the latest information and resources.

Joining an online forum like QRZ.com can also enhance your learning experience. QRZ.com is one of the largest amateur radio communities on the internet, featuring forums, a callsign database and educational resources. The forums cover a wide range of topics, including equipment reviews, technical support and general discussions about ham radio. Engaging in these discussions can provide insights and knowledge that you might not find elsewhere.

Facebook groups dedicated to Baofeng radios and amateur radio enthusiasts can be another valuable resource. Groups like "Baofeng Radio Users" and "Amateur Radio" are active communities where members post updates, share tips and provide support. These groups often host live Q&A sessions, share useful links and organize virtual meetups, which can help you stay engaged and informed.

For those interested in software programming for Baofeng radios, the CHIRP software website offers extensive documentation and user forums. CHIRP is a popular open-source tool for programming radios and its website provides downloads, user guides and a support forum. Engaging with the CHIRP community can help you understand how to customize your radio's settings and take full advantage of its capabilities.

The Ham Radio Deluxe software community is another excellent resource for those looking to enhance their radio communication experience. Ham Radio Deluxe offers a suite of software tools for radio control, logging and digital modes. Their website features tutorials, user manuals and a support forum where you can ask questions and share experiences with other users.

For international users, the IARU (International Amateur Radio Union) website provides information on global amateur radio activities, regulations and events. The IARU represents the interests of amateur radio operators worldwide and offers resources in multiple languages. Their website includes articles, news updates and links to regional organizations, making it a valuable resource for non-U.S. operators.

Engaging with local amateur radio clubs and organizations online can provide a more personalized learning experience. Many clubs have websites or social media pages where they post updates, event information and educational resources. Joining these online communities can help you connect with local enthusiasts, participate in virtual events and gain access to region-specific information and support.

There are numerous online resources, forums, and communities that can help you continue learning about Baofeng radios and two-way communication. By exploring these platforms, you can deepen your knowledge, stay updated on the latest developments and connect with a supportive community of fellow enthusiasts. Whether you prefer reading articles, watching videos or participating in discussions, these resources offer a wealth of information to help you make the most of your Baofeng radio.

CHAPTER 9

Enhancing Range and Performance

Optimizing Antenna Placement and Selection

Optimizing antenna placement and selecting the right type of antenna are crucial steps in enhancing the range and performance of your Baofeng radio. By understanding the principles behind antenna functionality and making informed choices, you can significantly improve your radio's communication capabilities.

Antenna placement is vital for maximizing signal strength and range. When positioning your antenna, aim for the highest and most unobstructed location possible. This is because radio signals travel in straight lines and can be blocked or weakened by obstacles such as buildings, trees and terrain. Placing your antenna on the roof of a building or on a tall mast can help ensure it has a clear line of sight, which enhances its ability to send and receive signals over greater distances.

Another important factor in antenna placement is the environment. Urban areas with many buildings and metallic structures can cause reflections and multipath interference, leading to signal degradation. In such settings, elevating the antenna above the surrounding structures can minimize these issues. Conversely, in rural or open areas, the primary consideration is height, as there are fewer obstructions. Ensuring that your antenna is higher than the immediate surroundings will maximize its range.

The type of antenna you choose also plays a significant role in performance. There are several types of antennas suitable for Baofeng radios, each with its own advantages. The most common types include the rubber duck antenna, whip antenna and high-gain antenna.

The rubber duck antenna is the standard antenna that comes with most handheld radios. It is short and flexible, making it convenient for portable use. However, it offers limited range compared to other options. For improved performance, consider upgrading to a whip antenna. Whip antennas are longer and more rigid, providing better signal reception and transmission due to their increased length. They are particularly useful for outdoor activities where you need a more robust connection.

High-gain antennas are another excellent option for enhancing range. These antennas are designed to focus the radio signal in a specific direction, increasing the effective transmission and reception distance. They are ideal for situations where you need to communicate over long distances or in areas with significant obstacles. However, high-gain antennas are usually larger and may require a more permanent installation setup.

In addition to selecting the right type of antenna, using an external antenna can further boost your radio's performance. External antennas are mounted outside of buildings or vehicles and connected to your radio via a coaxial cable. They are typically larger and can be positioned at higher elevations, providing superior range and signal clarity compared to handheld antennas. For mobile use, a magnetic mount antenna placed on the roof of your car can enhance communication while on the move.

Understanding the polarization of your antenna is also important. Most handheld radios use vertically polarized antennas, meaning the radio waves are oriented vertically. For optimal performance, ensure that all radios in your communication network use the same polarization. Mismatched polarization can result in significant signal loss. If you are using an external antenna, aligning it vertically or horizontally based on the polarization of the other antennas in your network will help maintain signal integrity.

Cable quality and length are additional considerations when optimizing antenna performance. The coaxial cable that connects your radio to an external antenna should be of high quality and as short as possible. Longer cables introduce signal loss, which can reduce the overall effectiveness of your antenna setup. Investing in low-loss coaxial cables can mitigate this issue, ensuring that more of your radio's power reaches the antenna and that incoming signals are received more clearly.

Another tip for maximizing antenna performance is to regularly inspect and maintain your antenna and connections. Over time, exposure to the elements can cause wear and tear on antennas, cables and connectors. Regularly checking for damage and ensuring all connections are secure can prevent signal loss and maintain optimal performance. Cleaning the antenna and connectors can also help, as dirt and corrosion can impede signal transmission.

In some cases, using a signal amplifier, or booster, can enhance your radio's range. These devices amplify the signal coming from your radio before it reaches the antenna, thereby increasing the effective communication distance. However, it's essential to use amplifiers that are compatible with your radio and adhere to legal transmission power limits set by regulatory authorities to avoid interference with other communications.

Consider the frequency band you are using. Baofeng radios typically operate on VHF (Very High Frequency) and UHF (Ultra High Frequency) bands. VHF signals travel farther and are better at penetrating foliage and other non-metallic obstacles, making them suitable for outdoor and rural environments. UHF signals, on the other hand, are better at penetrating buildings and urban structures but have a shorter range. Understanding the characteristics of these frequency bands can help you choose the best antenna and placement strategy for your specific communication needs.

Optimizing antenna placement and selection involves a combination of strategic positioning, choosing the right type of antenna, maintaining equipment and understanding the characteristics of your operating environment. By carefully considering these factors, you can significantly enhance the range and performance of your Baofeng radio, ensuring reliable communication whether you are in an urban setting, rural area or on the move.

Using Signal Boosters and Repeaters

Using signal boosters and repeaters can significantly extend the range of Baofeng radios, enhancing their effectiveness for both casual use and critical communication needs. By understanding how these devices work and following proper installation and usage practices, you can maximize your radio's performance.

Signal boosters, also known as amplifiers, are devices that increase the power of a radio signal, thereby extending its reach. When a radio transmits a signal, a booster amplifies this signal before it reaches the antenna, ensuring that it can travel further distances. Similarly, when receiving a signal, a booster enhances the incoming signal's strength, making it clearer and more reliable. Boosters are particularly useful in environments where obstacles or long distances can weaken signals, such as urban areas with many buildings or rural areas with vast open spaces.

Installing a signal booster involves several steps. First, you need to choose a booster compatible with your Baofeng radio's frequency range. Most Baofeng radios operate on VHF and UHF frequencies, so ensure the booster supports these bands. Once you have the right booster, connect it to your radio using a coaxial cable. Place the booster as close to the antenna as possible to minimize signal loss. Ensure all connections are secure to avoid interference and maintain signal quality.

Powering the booster is another crucial step. Most signal boosters require an external power source. Ensure you have a reliable power supply and if using the booster in a mobile setup, consider options like car battery adapters. Follow the manufacturer's instructions for connecting the power source to avoid damaging the booster or your radio equipment.

Repeaters are another powerful tool for extending the range of Baofeng radios. Unlike boosters, which amplify signals, repeaters receive a signal on one frequency and retransmit it on another, effectively doubling the distance the signal can travel. Repeaters are typically used in fixed locations, such as on tall buildings or towers, where they can provide wide-area coverage.

Setting up a repeater involves several considerations. First, select a suitable location. The higher the placement, the better the coverage area. Ensure the location has a clear line of sight to the areas you want to cover, minimizing obstacles like buildings or hills that could block the signal. Once you've chosen a location, mount the repeater securely, following the manufacturer's guidelines.

Next, configure the repeater's frequencies. A repeater operates by receiving a signal on one frequency, known as the input frequency and retransmitting it on another, known as the output frequency. Ensure these frequencies are appropriately spaced apart to avoid feedback or interference. Programming these frequencies into your Baofeng radio is crucial so that it can communicate effectively with the repeater.

Connecting the repeater to antennas is another critical step. Repeaters usually require two antennas: one for receiving and one for transmitting. These antennas should be placed as far apart as possible to prevent interference. Use high-quality coaxial cables to connect the antennas to the repeater and ensure all connections are tight and weatherproofed if the installation is outdoors.

Using a repeater with your Baofeng radio involves programming the radio with the repeater's input and output frequencies. This process varies slightly depending on your radio model, but generally, you will need to access the programming mode, enter the frequencies and save the settings. Ensure you also configure any required offset and tone settings, such as CTCSS or DCS codes, which are often used to access repeaters.

Maintaining both boosters and repeaters is essential for long-term performance. Regularly check connections and cables for wear and tear and replace any damaged components promptly. Keep the equipment clean and protected from environmental factors like rain or extreme temperatures. For repeaters, periodic checks to ensure they are operating correctly and that the antenna placement remains optimal are advisable.

In addition to extending the range, both boosters and repeaters improve signal clarity and reliability. In emergency situations, where communication is critical, having a robust setup with these devices can make a significant difference. They ensure that messages are transmitted and received clearly, reducing the risk of misunderstandings or missed communications.

Legal considerations are also important when using signal boosters and repeaters. Ensure that your use complies with local regulations and licensing requirements. In many regions, using repeaters and high-power boosters may require specific licenses. Check with your local communications authority to understand the regulations and obtain the necessary permissions.

For effective community use, setting up a repeater network can be beneficial. This involves coordinating with other radio users in your area to establish a series of repeaters that provide comprehensive coverage. Such networks can enhance communication for groups like emergency responders, event coordinators and neighborhood watch programs.

Signal boosters and repeaters are invaluable tools for extending the range and improving the performance of Baofeng radios. By carefully selecting, installing and maintaining these devices, you can ensure reliable and clear communication over greater distances. Whether for personal use, community activities or emergency preparedness, understanding and utilizing boosters and repeaters effectively can greatly enhance your radio communication capabilities.

Environmental Factors Affecting Signal Strength

Environmental factors play a significant role in the performance and reliability of Baofeng radios. Understanding how terrain, weather, and obstacles affect signal strength can help users optimize their communication strategies. By being aware of these influences and implementing strategies to mitigate their effects, users can ensure more consistent and clear transmissions.

Terrain is one of the most critical factors influencing radio signal strength. Radio waves travel in straight lines and can be obstructed by hills, mountains and other natural formations. For example, in mountainous regions, signals may be blocked or reflected, leading to weak or unreliable communication. To mitigate these issues, it is essential to position yourself in a location with a clear line of sight to the person you are communicating with. Elevating your position, such as moving to a higher ground or using a taller antenna, can help overcome some of the terrain-related challenges. Additionally, using repeaters placed at high altitudes can extend the range by retransmitting the signal over obstacles.

Weather conditions also impact radio signals. Rain, snow and fog can absorb and scatter radio waves, reducing their strength and clarity. Moisture in the air, especially in the form of heavy rain or dense fog, can significantly attenuate high-frequency signals. Cold weather can affect battery performance, causing the radio to lose power more quickly. To mitigate weather-related issues, consider using weather-resistant equipment and ensuring that your radio and accessories are properly protected from moisture. When planning outdoor activities, be aware of the weather forecast and plan your communication strategy accordingly. In extreme cold, keep spare batteries warm and close to your body to maintain their charge.

Obstacles, both natural and man-made, can obstruct radio signals. Buildings, trees and vehicles can block or reflect signals, leading to dead zones where communication is impossible. In urban environments, where buildings are dense, signal strength can be particularly affected. To overcome these challenges, use higher-gain antennas, which can focus the signal more narrowly and penetrate obstacles more effectively. Positioning antennas on rooftops or other elevated structures can also help avoid obstructions. Additionally, when communicating in an environment with many obstacles, consider using repeaters strategically placed to bridge gaps in coverage.

The density and type of vegetation can also affect signal strength. Dense forests with thick canopies can absorb and scatter radio waves, weakening the signal. In contrast, open fields and sparsely wooded areas allow for better signal propagation. When operating in heavily forested areas, using higher frequencies (like UHF) can sometimes be beneficial, as they can penetrate foliage more effectively than lower frequencies (like VHF). However, UHF signals are generally more susceptible to attenuation by obstacles, so balancing frequency choice with environmental conditions is crucial.

Urban environments present unique challenges due to the abundance of reflective surfaces and electronic interference. Tall buildings can create multipath interference, where signals bounce off surfaces and arrive at the receiver at slightly different times, causing distortion. Additionally, electronic devices such as Wi-Fi routers, microwave ovens and even other radios can create interference. To mitigate these effects, use radios with good noise rejection capabilities and avoid frequencies commonly used by other electronic devices. Employing digital modes of communication, which are less susceptible to interference and signal degradation, can also improve clarity in urban settings.

Temperature inversions, a weather phenomenon where a layer of warm air traps a layer of cooler air near the ground, can cause unusual signal propagation. This condition can create "ducting," where signals travel much farther than normal, potentially causing interference with distant stations. While this can sometimes be beneficial for extending range, it can also lead to unexpected communication issues. Being aware of such weather patterns and adjusting your communication strategy accordingly can help manage these anomalies.

For effective communication in environments with significant environmental challenges, having a flexible setup and being prepared to adjust your equipment and strategy is essential. Carrying a variety of antennas, including portable high-gain antennas, can help adapt to different conditions. Using a mix of simplex and duplex communication methods, where simplex involves direct communication between radios and duplex involves using repeaters, can also provide more reliable coverage.

In emergency situations, where reliable communication is crucial, understanding the impact of environmental factors is particularly important. Pre-planning and conducting regular drills in various conditions can help identify potential issues and develop effective mitigation strategies. Having backup equipment, such as additional batteries, signal boosters and portable repeaters, ensures that you are prepared for unexpected challenges.

Environmental factors such as terrain, weather, and obstacles significantly impact the performance of Baofeng radios. By understanding these influences and implementing strategies to mitigate their effects, users can enhance the reliability and clarity of their communications. Whether in urban environments, dense forests or open fields, being prepared and adaptable is key to maintaining effective communication. Employing the right equipment, positioning and techniques will help overcome the challenges posed by environmental factors, ensuring that your Baofeng radio performs optimally in any situation.

DIY Projects for Improving Radio Performance

Improving the performance of Baofeng radios can be an engaging and rewarding experience. With a few do-it-yourself (DIY) projects and modifications, you can significantly enhance the capabilities of your radio, ensuring better communication range, clarity and overall functionality. These projects range from simple antenna upgrades to more complex modifications that involve tweaking the internal components of the radio. Here are several detailed DIY projects to help you get started.

One of the most effective ways to improve your Baofeng radio's performance is by upgrading the antenna. The stock antennas that come with

Baofeng radios are often basic and can be improved upon. A popular upgrade is replacing the stock antenna with a longer, high-gain antenna. Antennas like the Nagoya NA-771 or Diamond SRJ77CA are widely recommended by enthusiasts for their superior performance. These antennas are simple to attach; just unscrew the old antenna and screw in the new one. This upgrade can significantly enhance both transmission and reception capabilities, especially in challenging environments.

For those who want to go a step further, building a custom antenna can provide even greater performance improvements. One popular DIY project is constructing a roll-up J-pole antenna using ladder line or twin-lead cable. The J-pole antenna is known for its excellent omnidirectional reception and ease of construction. To build one, you will need a length of ladder line, a coaxial cable with a connector that matches your radio and some basic tools like a soldering iron. By following online tutorials and diagrams, you can cut and solder the ladder line to the appropriate lengths, attach the coaxial cable and create an antenna that can be easily rolled up and transported.

Improving the grounding of your Baofeng radio can also enhance performance, especially for stationary use. Poor grounding can lead to increased noise and reduced signal clarity. For a simple DIY grounding project, you can create a counterpoise, also known as a "tiger tail." This involves attaching a length of wire to the ground side of your antenna connector. The wire should be approximately the same length as your antenna and can be wrapped around the base of the antenna or connected directly to the radio's chassis. This counterpoise acts as an artificial ground plane, improving signal transmission and reception.

Another effective DIY project is adding an external microphone and speaker. The built-in microphone and speaker on Baofeng radios are functional but can be limiting in noisy environments or when clarity is crucial. External microphones and speakers can be purchased relatively cheaply and provide much clearer audio. You can also create your own custom setups by modifying existing microphones and speakers. This might involve soldering connectors that match your radio's input/output ports and possibly constructing enclosures to house the components for better durability and sound quality.

For users who are comfortable with more advanced modifications, enhancing the power output of your Baofeng radio can be a worthwhile project. This involves modifying the internal circuitry to increase the radio's wattage. However, it is important to note that this can be complex and may void any warranty on the device. Additionally, increasing power output can lead to regulatory compliance issues, so it is crucial to understand the legal limits in your area. If you decide to proceed, you will need detailed schematics of your radio model and experience with electronic soldering and component replacement.

Customizing the user interface of your Baofeng radio can also improve usability. Many Baofeng models allow for firmware upgrades and custom programming through software like Chirp. By connecting your radio to a computer via a programming cable, you can download and install updated firmware that may provide new features and improved performance. Additionally, using Chirp software, you can program custom frequency lists, channel names and settings, tailoring the radio's functionality to your specific needs. This project requires downloading the necessary software, installing the appropriate drivers, and following programming guides specific to your radio model.

For outdoor enthusiasts, creating a durable protective case can ensure that your Baofeng radio remains functional in harsh conditions. This DIY project involves repurposing a waterproof container, such as a Pelican case and customizing it to fit your radio and accessories. By adding foam inserts, you can secure the radio and prevent damage from impacts and moisture. Some users also install external ports in the case for antennas and microphones, allowing the radio to be used without removing it from the protective enclosure.

Improving the battery performance of your Baofeng radio can be achieved through a couple of DIY modifications. One simple project is creating a battery pack using rechargeable AA or 18650 lithium-ion batteries. These battery packs can be constructed using battery holders and appropriate wiring, providing a longer-lasting power source compared to the standard battery pack. Additionally, adding a solar charging setup can ensure that your radio remains operational even in remote locations. This involves connecting a small solar panel to a charge controller and the radio's battery pack, allowing for sustainable off-grid operation.

Constructing a signal amplifier or booster can significantly enhance your radio's range. This project is more complex and involves creating a circuit that amplifies the radio signal before it is transmitted. Kits and components for building signal amplifiers are available online, but this modification requires a good understanding of radio frequency electronics and careful adherence to design specifications to avoid damaging your radio or violating transmission power regulations.

There are numerous DIY projects and modifications that can improve the performance of Baofeng radios. From simple antenna upgrades to more complex internal modifications, each project can enhance different aspects of the radio's capabilities. By carefully selecting and implementing these modifications, users can tailor their radios to better meet their specific needs and operating environments, ensuring reliable and effective communication in a variety of situations.

CHAPTER 10

Future Trends and Innovations in Radio Communication

The Impact of Digital Modes on Two-Way Radios

Digital communication modes are revolutionizing the field of two-way radios, bringing numerous advancements that promise to shape the future of radio communication. These digital modes enhance audio clarity, improve data transmission and offer features that analog radios simply cannot match. Understanding the impact of these modes and staying informed about current trends can provide a glimpse into the future possibilities of two-way radio technology.

One of the most significant advantages of digital modes over analog is audio clarity. Digital radios use advanced signal processing to filter out background noise and interference, resulting in clearer and more reliable communication. This is particularly important in noisy environments or situations where precise communication is crucial. Digital radios can maintain clarity over greater distances, whereas analog signals tend to degrade and become noisy as distance increases.

Digital modes also enable better data transmission capabilities. In addition to voice communication, digital radios can send and receive text messages, GPS coordinates and other types of data. This feature is especially useful in emergency situations, allowing for the transmission of critical information even when voice communication is impractical. For example, rescue teams can share their exact locations and organizations can broadcast alerts and instructions efficiently.

Encryption and security are other areas where digital modes excel. Digital radios can employ sophisticated encryption algorithms to protect communications from eavesdropping. This is a significant advantage for military, law enforcement and private sector users who need to ensure that their communications remain confidential. The ability to encrypt data and voice transmissions helps prevent unauthorized access and maintains the integrity of sensitive information.

The transition from analog to digital is facilitated by standards such as Digital Mobile Radio (DMR) and Project 25 (P25). These standards provide frameworks for interoperability between different manufacturers and ensure that radios can communicate with each other regardless of the brand. This interoperability is critical for large-scale operations involving multiple agencies and organizations, such as disaster response and public safety coordination.

Current trends in digital two-way radios include the integration of Internet Protocol (IP) connectivity, which allows radios to connect to the internet and other IP-based networks. This integration opens up new possibilities for communication, such as connecting radios across vast distances using the internet or linking radio networks with other communication systems like smartphones and computers. This connectivity also supports remote management and programming, enabling users to update and configure their radios without needing physical access.

Another emerging trend is the miniaturization and ruggedization of digital radios. Advances in technology are allowing manufacturers to produce smaller, lighter and more durable radios without sacrificing performance. These compact devices are ideal for use in harsh environments and by personnel who need to remain mobile. For example, modern digital radios can withstand extreme temperatures, moisture and physical shocks, making them suitable for military and industrial applications.

The development of software-defined radios (SDRs) is a promising innovation that could significantly impact the future of two-way radios. SDRs use software to perform many of the functions traditionally handled by hardware, making them highly flexible and upgradable. With SDR technology, users can update their radios with new features and capabilities simply by downloading software updates. This flexibility allows radios to adapt to evolving communication standards and user needs without requiring new hardware.

Artificial intelligence (AI) and machine learning are also beginning to influence the field of radio communication. AI algorithms can enhance signal processing, optimize frequency use, and manage network resources more efficiently. For example, AI can dynamically adjust transmission power and frequency to minimize interference and maximize signal quality. Machine learning can also analyze communication patterns and predict network congestion, allowing for proactive management and better overall performance.

Looking to the future, the convergence of radio communication with other technologies such as augmented reality (AR) and the Internet of Things (IoT) presents exciting possibilities. AR can provide users with visual overlays of communication data, such as showing the locations of team members on a heads-up display. IoT integration allows radios to communicate with a wide range of smart devices, creating a more interconnected and responsive communication environment. For instance, a Baofeng radio could automatically adjust its settings based on the user's location and environmental conditions.

Digital communication modes are significantly enhancing the functionality and reliability of two-way radios. The benefits of digital modes, such as improved audio clarity, data transmission, encryption, and interoperability are driving the transition from analog to digital. Emerging trends like IP connectivity, miniaturization, ruggedization, software-defined radios and the integration of AI and machine learning are poised to further transform the field. As these technologies continue to evolve, the future of two-way radio communication looks increasingly interconnected, intelligent and versatile.

Integration with Smartphones and Other Devices

Integrating Baofeng radios with smartphones and other devices enhances communication capabilities and offers a range of practical applications. This integration leverages the strengths of both traditional two-way radios and modern digital devices, creating a versatile and efficient communication network. There are several ways to achieve this integration, each with unique benefits and use cases.

One of the most straightforward methods for integrating Baofeng radios with smartphones is through the use of a cable or adapter that connects the radio's audio output to the smartphone's audio input. This setup allows the smartphone to act as an interface for the radio, enabling the user to transmit and receive audio through the radio while using the smartphone's speaker and microphone. This method is simple and effective for basic communication needs, such as during outdoor activities or emergency situations.

Another popular method involves using Bluetooth adapters. These adapters can be attached to Baofeng radios, enabling wireless communication between the radio and a smartphone. Bluetooth adapters are especially useful for users who need hands-free operation, such as hikers, cyclists or security personnel. By connecting the radio to a smartphone via Bluetooth, users can keep their hands free while still maintaining clear communication with their team.

Smartphone applications designed for radio integration offer even more advanced functionality. Apps like Zello and EchoLink allow smartphones to interface with two-way radios over the internet. These apps convert the smartphone into a virtual walkie-talkie, enabling users to communicate with radio operators anywhere in the world, provided there is internet connectivity. For instance, Zello allows users to create channels for specific groups, making it easy to coordinate activities or manage large events. EchoLink, on the other hand, connects ham radio operators worldwide, facilitating long-distance communication and international collaborations.

Integration with smartphones also enables the use of GPS and mapping features to enhance radio communication. By connecting a Baofeng radio to a smartphone, users can share their GPS coordinates with others in their group. This feature is particularly useful for outdoor adventurers, search and rescue teams and event organizers. For example, during a hiking expedition, team members can see each other's locations on a map in real-time, ensuring that no one gets lost and allowing for quick coordination in case of an emergency.

Smartphone integration also allows for the recording and logging of radio communications. Apps can record conversations transmitted through the radio, providing a record of communication that can be reviewed later. This feature is beneficial for security teams, event coordinators and emergency responders who need to keep detailed records of their operations. Recorded communications can be used for training purposes, incident reviews and legal documentation.

In addition to smartphones, Baofeng radios can be integrated with other digital devices, such as tablets and computers. This integration is particularly useful in command centers or control rooms where multiple communication channels need to be monitored simultaneously. Software applications designed for desktops and tablets can interface with Baofeng radios, allowing operators to manage radio traffic, coordinate teams and communicate with field personnel from a centralized location. This setup enhances operational efficiency and situational awareness.

For amateur radio enthusiasts, integrating Baofeng radios with computers opens up a world of possibilities. Software-defined radio (SDR) programs, such as Ham Radio Deluxe and SDR Console, can be used to control Baofeng radios from a computer. These programs offer advanced features like spectrum analysis, digital mode operation and logging, making it easier for ham radio operators to experiment with different frequencies and communication modes. By connecting the radio to a computer, users can also participate in digital communication modes like

PSK31, RTTY and FT8, which are popular in the amateur radio community.

Another exciting application of Baofeng radio integration is in the realm of the Internet of Things (IoT). By connecting Baofeng radios to IoT devices, users can create automated systems that enhance communication and safety. For example, IoT sensors can be used to monitor environmental conditions and automatically transmit alerts via the radio when certain thresholds are exceeded. This setup is useful in industrial settings, where monitoring conditions such as temperature, humidity and gas levels is critical for safety. Similarly, home automation systems can use Baofeng radios to send alerts in case of security breaches or emergencies.

In the field of public safety, integrating Baofeng radios with digital devices can improve coordination and response times. Police, fire and medical services can use integrated systems to share real-time information, such as incident locations, status updates and resource allocation. By using tablets or smartphones connected to Baofeng radios, first responders can access critical information while on the move, enhancing their ability to make informed decisions and respond effectively to emergencies.

The educational sector also benefits from the integration of Baofeng radios with digital devices. Schools and universities can use integrated systems for campus security, event coordination and communication during emergencies. By connecting radios to a central communication hub, administrators can monitor and manage communication channels, ensuring that information is disseminated quickly and accurately during critical situations.

Integrating Baofeng radios with smartphones and other digital devices significantly enhances communication capabilities and offers a wide range of practical applications. Whether for outdoor adventures, emergency response, public safety or amateur radio experimentation, this integration provides users with the tools they need to stay connected and informed. By leveraging the strengths of both traditional radios and modern digital technology, users can create versatile and efficient communication networks tailored to their specific needs.

Emerging Technologies in Emergency Communication

Emerging technologies are constantly reshaping the landscape of emergency communication, bringing innovative solutions that promise to enhance the effectiveness of two-way radios and improve response times during critical situations. These technologies leverage advancements in areas such as connectivity, data processing and sensor integration to create more robust and resilient communication networks. Understanding these emerging technologies can provide valuable insights into the future of emergency communication and preparedness.

One of the most promising advancements in emergency communication is the integration of artificial intelligence (AI) and machine learning (ML) algorithms. These technologies can analyze vast amounts of data in real-time, allowing for more accurate prediction of emergencies and faster response times. For example, AI-powered systems can monitor social media, sensor networks and other data sources for early signs of disasters such as wildfires, floods or earthquakes. By analyzing patterns and trends, these systems can provide early warnings to emergency responders, enabling them to take proactive measures to mitigate the impact of the disaster.

Another area of innovation is the use of unmanned aerial vehicles (UAVs) or drones, for emergency communication. Drones equipped with communication equipment, such as repeaters or mobile base stations, can quickly establish temporary communication networks in areas where traditional infrastructure has been damaged or destroyed. These drones can fly over disaster zones, providing connectivity to first responders and affected communities, facilitating coordination and rescue efforts. Additionally, drones can be used for aerial reconnaissance, allowing emergency teams to assess the extent of damage and identify areas in need of assistance.

Satellite communication technology is also playing a crucial role in emergency communication, particularly in remote or isolated regions where terrestrial infrastructure is lacking. Satellite phones and satellite-based internet services provide reliable communication capabilities even in areas without cellular coverage or during natural disasters that disrupt terrestrial networks. These technologies enable emergency responders to maintain communication with command centers and coordinate rescue operations effectively, regardless of location or environmental conditions.

The Internet of Things (IoT) is another emerging technology with significant potential to improve emergency communication. IoT devices, such as sensors and smart sensors, can collect real-time data on environmental conditions, infrastructure status and human activity. This data can be transmitted wirelessly to a central monitoring system, where AI algorithms analyze it to detect anomalies or potential emergencies. For example, IoT sensors installed in buildings can monitor structural integrity and detect signs of damage or instability, alerting authorities to potential hazards before they escalate into emergencies.

In recent years, advances in wearable technology have also contributed to the improvement of emergency communication. Smartwatches, fitness trackers and other wearable devices equipped with communication capabilities can provide users with real-time alerts and notifications during emergencies. These devices can monitor vital signs, detect falls or accidents and automatically send distress signals to emergency contacts or authorities. For example, a hiker wearing a smartwatch equipped with GPS and cellular connectivity can quickly summon help in case of injury or getting lost in the wilderness.

Blockchain technology is another emerging trend that holds promise for enhancing emergency communication and response. Blockchain, a decentralized and secure digital ledger, can be used to store and verify critical information, such as emergency response protocols, medical records and supply chain logistics. By leveraging blockchain technology, emergency responders can ensure the integrity and authenticity of information shared across multiple agencies and organizations, improving coordination and decision-making during crises.

Advancements in augmented reality (AR) and virtual reality (VR) also have the potential to revolutionize emergency communication and training. AR and VR technologies can simulate realistic emergency scenarios, allowing responders to practice and refine their skills in a safe and controlled environment. For example, firefighters can use AR headsets to visualize building layouts, locate hazards and plan evacuation routes before entering a burning building. Similarly, medical personnel can use VR simulations to practice triage procedures and emergency medical interventions, improving their readiness to respond to mass casualty incidents.

Emerging technologies are transforming the field of emergency communication, offering innovative solutions that enhance the effectiveness of two-way radios and improve response times during crises. From AI-powered predictive analytics to drone-enabled communication networks, these technologies have the potential to revolutionize how emergency responders communicate, coordinate and collaborate during disasters and emergencies. By embracing these advancements and integrating them into existing communication infrastructure, we can build more resilient and adaptive emergency communication systems that save lives and mitigate the impact of disasters.

The Future of Baofeng and Other Affordable Radio Solutions

The future of Baofeng radios and other affordable radio solutions holds exciting potential, driven by advancements in technology, changes in consumer preferences and evolving market dynamics. As we look ahead, several key trends and developments are likely to shape the trajectory of these products, offering new opportunities and challenges for manufacturers, retailers and users alike.

One of the most significant trends driving the future of affordable radio solutions is the increasing demand for versatile and feature-rich communication devices at accessible price points. As technology continues to evolve and become more affordable, consumers are seeking radios that offer advanced functionalities without breaking the bank. Baofeng, known for its cost-effective yet capable radios, is well-positioned to capitalize on this trend by continuing to innovate and offer products that meet the needs of budget-conscious users.

In addition to affordability, convenience and ease of use are becoming increasingly important factors for consumers when choosing a radio solution. As such, we can expect to see continued efforts to streamline the user experience and simplify the operation of Baofeng radios and other affordable options. This may involve the development of intuitive interfaces, improved ergonomic designs and enhanced accessibility features to cater to users of all ages and abilities.

Another emerging trend in the affordable radio market is the integration of modern connectivity technologies, such as Bluetooth and Wi-Fi. By incorporating these features into their products, manufacturers like Baofeng can offer users more flexibility and versatility in how they communicate. For example, Bluetooth connectivity enables seamless pairing with smartphones and other devices, allowing for hands-free operation and integration with mobile apps. Wi-Fi connectivity, on the other hand, enables wireless data transfer and remote control capabilities, opening up new possibilities for remote monitoring and management of radio systems.

Furthermore, advancements in digital signal processing (DSP) and software-defined radio (SDR) technology are likely to drive innovation in affordable radio solutions. These technologies enable manufacturers to implement advanced features such as noise reduction, signal filtering and encryption, improving the clarity and reliability of communication in challenging environments. Baofeng and other manufacturers may leverage DSP and SDR technology to enhance the performance of their radios and differentiate their products in the market.

As the demand for affordable radio solutions continues to grow, we can also expect to see an expansion of the product ecosystem surrounding Baofeng and similar brands. This may include the development of a wide range of accessories and peripherals designed to enhance the functionality and versatility of these radios. Accessories such as antennas, battery packs, cases and mounting solutions can provide users with additional options for customizing and optimizing their radio systems to suit their specific needs and preferences.

Moreover, the future of affordable radio solutions is closely tied to broader trends in communication technology, including the emergence of 5G networks, the Internet of Things (IoT) and the proliferation of smart devices. Baofeng and other manufacturers may explore opportunities to integrate their radios with these technologies, enabling seamless connectivity and interoperability with other devices and systems. For example, Baofeng radios equipped with IoT sensors could provide real-time data on environmental conditions, infrastructure status and human activity, enhancing situational awareness and decision-making for users in various applications.

In terms of market dynamics, the affordable radio segment is expected to remain highly competitive, with new players entering the market and existing players expanding their product portfolios. Baofeng, as a market leader in this segment, will need to stay vigilant and responsive to evolving consumer preferences and market trends. This may involve investing in research and development to innovate new features and technologies, expanding distribution channels to reach new customers and maintaining strong customer relationships through responsive support and service.

The future of Baofeng radios and other affordable radio solutions is bright and full of possibilities. By leveraging advancements in technology, responding to changing consumer needs and adapting to evolving market dynamics, Baofeng and other manufacturers can continue to offer innovative and reliable communication solutions that empower users to stay connected, informed and safe in any situation. As affordability, convenience and performance remain key priorities for consumers, we can expect to see continued innovation and growth in this exciting segment of the communication market.

CONCLUSION

Radio communication is a skill that grows stronger with practice and continuous learning. Baofeng radios offer a fantastic opportunity to enhance this skill, but to truly master it, ongoing education is essential. Keep engaging with your radio regularly to build confidence and proficiency. Practice makes perfect and with every use, you'll become more adept at handling your device in various scenarios.

There are numerous resources to help you on this journey. Online forums and communities such as Reddit's r/baofeng or dedicated ham radio forums can provide a wealth of knowledge and support from fellow enthusiasts. YouTube channels and tutorial websites offer visual guides that can clarify complex functions and programming steps. Additionally, consider joining local radio clubs where you can participate in hands-on activities and learn from experienced operators.

Ham radio events, such as field days and contests, are also excellent opportunities to practice your skills and learn new techniques. Participating in these events can expose you to different aspects of radio communication and help you build a network of like-minded individuals who share your passion.

Understanding and effectively using your Baofeng radio can significantly enhance your communication capabilities. Here are some final tips to help you get the most out of your device:

Read the Manual: It might seem obvious, but the manual that comes with your Baofeng radio is a valuable resource. It provides detailed information about the features and functions specific to your model.

Regular Maintenance: Keep your radio clean and dry to ensure it works correctly. Wipe it down regularly and check for any signs of wear or damage. A well-maintained radio is more reliable and has a longer lifespan.

Practice Key Functions: Spend time practicing basic and advanced functions like programming channels, using repeater channels and setting up dual watch modes. Familiarity with these functions will make you more efficient during actual use.

Upgrade Antennas: The stock antenna that comes with your Baofeng radio is adequate for general use, but upgrading to a higher-quality antenna can significantly improve your range and signal clarity. Consider investing in a reputable aftermarket antenna.

Use Quality Accessories: Accessories like earpieces, external microphones and battery packs can enhance your radio experience. Choose accessories that are compatible with your Baofeng model to ensure the best performance.

Monitor Local Frequencies: Stay tuned to local frequencies for updates on weather, emergencies and community activities. This habit keeps you informed and prepared for any situation that might arise.

Stay Legal: Always adhere to local regulations regarding radio communication. Ensure you have the necessary licenses if required and use your radio responsibly to avoid interference with public services.

Participate in Drills: Engage in community or club-organized drills to simulate emergency scenarios. These drills can help you practice your skills in a controlled environment and prepare you for real-life situations.

Learn Morse Code: Although not mandatory, learning Morse code can be a valuable skill. It's an effective form of communication, especially in emergencies where voice communication might not be possible.

Experiment with Different Settings: Don't be afraid to explore and experiment with your radio's settings. Trying out different frequencies, modes and configurations can help you discover the best setups for various situations.

Document Your Learnings: Keep a log of frequencies, settings, and experiences. This log can serve as a quick reference and help you remember effective strategies and configurations.

Stay Connected: Use your radio to stay in touch with family, friends and community members, especially in emergencies. Regular check-ins ensure that everyone is safe and informed.

By incorporating these tips into your routine, you can maximize the potential of your Baofeng radio. Embracing the power of communication means not only understanding the technical aspects but also fostering a spirit of continuous learning and practice. With dedication and the right resources, you'll be well-equipped to handle any communication needs, whether for everyday use or during critical situations.

www.ingramcontent.com/pod-product-compliance
Lightning Source LLC
Chambersburg PA
CBHW050050230526
45470CB00004B/1471